Adeline Dutton Train Whitney

Patience Strong's Outings

Adeline Dutton Train Whitney

Patience Strong's Outings

ISBN/EAN: 9783743301429

Manufactured in Europe, USA, Canada, Australia, Japa

Cover: Foto ©ninafisch / pixelio.de

Manufactured and distributed by brebook publishing software (www.brebook.com)

Adeline Dutton Train Whitney

Patience Strong's Outings

PATIENCE STRONG'S OUTINGS.

BY

MRS. A. D. T. WHITNEY,

AUTHOR OF "FAITH GARTNEY'S GIRLHOOD," "THE GAYWORTHYS," ETC., ETC.

LORING, Publisher,
COR. BROMFIELD AND WASHINGTON STREETS,
BOSTON.

CONTENTS.

CHAPTER	PAGE
I — INTO THE BY-GONES	7
II. — STILLNESS AND STITCHES	18
III. — THE COMINGS-IN	26
IV. — THE LIFE AND THE GLORY	41
V. — INTO THE MEANINGS	54
VI. — INTO THE OLD AND THE NEW	67
VII. — "FORZINO"	79
VIII. — INTO DARK CLOSETS AND NEIGHBOR-HOUSES	92
IX. — INTO THE MIDDLES	105
X. — INTO THE SUNSHINE	113
XI. — INTO THE SHOPS	122
XII. — INTO THE YEARS	135

CONTENTS.

CHAPTER	PAGE
XIII.—INTO THE NEW TESTAMENT PART OF IT	143
XIV.—INTO GOD'S TREASURE-BOX	157
XV.—INTO THE FAIRY STORY	168
XVI.—WITH THE SUNDAY STRAYS	180
XVII.—INTO OTHER PEOPLE'S BUSINESS	193
XVIII.—INTO THE MIDNIGHT	208
XIX.—INTO THE DAY-GLEAM	209
XX.—INTO THE MORNING	221

Patience Strong's Outings.

I.

INTO THE BY-GONES.

"Eliphalet's folks are going to Europe."

Mother says that in a meek kind of way, trying not to be too much set up about it, to the neighbors when they come in, and ask, as the neighbors here have a way of doing, "What the good word is with us?"

It makes me think, — that greeting, — always. It seems, somehow, as if it were a sweet old fashion that might have come down out of the kingdom of heaven.

That syllable is so full, — "word!" That which "was in the beginning with God," and "without which nothing was made that is made." What he has been giving out, always, — down, through the angels, unto men, and into things. God's meanings, of thought and of life; his instant bestowal.

Looking at it so, it is tender and solemn to hear the neighbors ask, "What the good word is to-day?" And to hear mother say, with that kind of tremble in her voice that she tries to straighten into calmness, "Eliphalet's folks are going to Europe,"—why, it is as if the leave for the pleasure *was* just the day's word from God.

I know mother is glad and proud at Eliphalet's well-doing and getting-on. She is a little afraid of his wife, because she belongs to a Boston family of consequence, and is very elegant in her manners, and never takes them off, not even for the most common every-day. But then, as mother says, she isn't "stuck-up," because she never *got* up, and she never comes down. She was always just so. She is very respectful and kind to mother, but she don't like to be introduced as "Eliphalet's wife." She is "my daughter-in-law, Mrs. Strong." Not even "Mrs. Eliphalet" since father died, though she was particular about that before. She never objected nor suggested in so many words; but we always find out, somehow, just what Gertrude considers proper, and likes to be done. She is "Gertrude" among us. *Mother* wouldn't like it otherwise; and mother has her quiet proprieties too.

Well, Eliphalet's folks are going to Europe. He and Gertrude, and the children, and their nurse, and their Aunt Marthe. (That is not a Yankee shortening; the French terminal makes all the difference in the prettiness. It is just so with other words. I remember that I would not call my white waists "gamps," thinking of bed-gowns and Sairey; but when I found out that it was the French "guimpe," it gave a grace to the name and the thing. I don't know why we *shouldn't* be graceful, even if we have to be French.)

Everybody goes to Europe now. I think it is to get rid of the kitchens. There are two currents in the Atlantic,— an upper and a lower. The tide comes in at our basement stories, and has to flow out again at the parlor and front doors. Perhaps that is the reason the Gulf Stream is changing. Things have to equalize and accommodate.

Eliphalet came out last Sunday evening on horseback and took tea, and told mother all about it. They are to stay a year or more; travel in England and

Scotland, and Switzerland this summer, and then go to Italy for the winter, and, in the spring come to Paris; home when they get ready. How much that is, to do and to see! I wonder if those little children will take in anything, out of it all, to keep.

"Pashie, *you* ought to go too. You don't get many outings."

Eliphalet said that just as he went off, when I was bidding him good-by, standing on the door-step, patting his horse's nose, and giving him mouthfuls of fresh clover out of my hand.

Don't I have many outings?

It has been in my head ever since. I don't think Eliphalet knows. It depends upon how far you *go* out when your gate's ajar. Everybody's little yard-room opens into all out-doors.

Why it seems to me that life is *all* outings. When you don't go out any longer, you die. There's no such thing as shutting people up.

Mother and I have lived here, all by ourselves, for ten years. Before that, we had father to take care of for five years, from the time he first had paralysis.

And before that it was Aunt Judith, and she was deaf, and dreadfully, — well, *unexpected* in her ways. I'm thirty-eight now, and mother's fifty-six. My dear, little, young-old mother! I am her oldest. So near her! I am so glad. We're such comforts to each other.

Why I've all her life to go out into, in the first place. Ever since she used to tell me stories about "when she was little," and "when she was young."

She keeps that dear, simple way of speaking that she learned when she was "little," and when she was "young," from *her* mother and the old-time friends. And yet she has gone on with the years, to take in and enjoy what the years teach. She knows new books, and new thoughts, and the light of to-day on old things shines for her as truly as for any one. We talk over the philosophers together, she and I; and we love the grand speculations that take in the ideas of a humanity hundreds of thousands of years old, and the earths buried within the earth; its coarse, wild, rudimentary, seething, passionate Past, rank and slimy and ravenous with wilderness and reptile and beast, covered up and softened over, and changed; greened and beautified, and peopled with fairer and fairer life, telling us, in a Word as big as the world, of how it shall be with men's souls in the long time and patience that God is rich in.

She loves all this, but she does not trouble about new phrases and pronunciations in her every-day speech. She says " our folks " — (kindly old Anglo-Saxon) — where Gertrude would say " our family, " or " my father's family ; " and she speaks of when she was " little," so that it makes you feel tender toward the little child that she was, and that somewhere in her nature she has not yet ceased to be. She " suffers the little child " in herself, and is in nowise ashamed of it, and by it she does always behold the Father's face. My dear, little, young-old mother! That is the heart-word I always have for her, and that is how I call her.

There were so many of them, sisters, once ; and her life takes me back into all their lives. Now, there are only mother and Aunt Hetty Maria.

Aunt Hetty Maria married the two largest and oldest farms in Dearwood together ; and her husband has been a member of Congress, and she lives at the old homestead, and is a great deal thought of and looked up to. She always wears black silk in the afternoons; and when people come to see her they put on their best, in gowns and in behavior; and her tea-table is always ready for company, and set with real china, that you can see through. Somebody almost always does come in to tea in the summer time, and so her house is "society" for Dearwood. To take tea at Madam Parmenter's is to take the best thing at once, and the freedom of all there is. The ministers always go there, and the lecturers, and people that have any public business, and those who have friends staying with them.

It is very quiet and old-fashioned and dignified there now. It has got the air that only ripens with a hundred years' living. But those are the rooms they were born and grew up in, and were married out of, — those who were married; buried out of, — those who died; and there was where the young folks had their tea-drinkings and their courtings, and their housefuls of friends at Thanksgivings and holiday-times; and their garden and orchard walks and talks when the damask roses were in bloom or the peaches were ripe; and their moonlight sittings under the great trees at the wide front door.

I have all that when I go to Dearwood. It is all there; and that is one of my outings. Many avenued, into the lives that have been partly told me, and that have partly told themselves. I never stand at the landing half-way up the broad, shallow-stepped staircase, but I seem to feel how it was when they and their visitors went up to bed in the old times; when they stood there with shining candlesticks in their hands, and called up and down to each other in the last talk and laugh of the night, which is always the brightest and most beguiling. Nobody ever said a word about that; but I know it by what they would call, nowadays, psychometry, I suppose.

Aunt Hetty Maria's picture hangs in the parlor. It's a picture of gown and great white ruffled cape, mostly; the features are of little account, and were never thought to look much like her. But I like it for the very gown and cape, such as they don't wear now even in their dreams. Such things grow queer in a portrait for a while, and then they grow ancient and graphic. Then they tell stories, and are as much as a face. They become the things that *portray*.

It makes me think of warm, pleasant weather, and company coming, that picture, with the low-necked silk gown, and the wide, clear, fresh muslin cape, with the ruffles standing off at the shoulders, and the hair done up in high, smooth bows. It wouldn't have been a dress to play croquet, or Aunt Sally, or ship-coil in; but to talk, and walk, and gather roses, and sit in state in the best parlor for a hand-round tea; and so, when I stand and look at it, it takes me right back to itself and into its day.

Why, there are plenty of ways to get *out!* Away out into the long-lived years, with people one never saw or knew. An old house, an old picture, a word in a book can do it. One needn't necessarily cross the water. If one does, it is to get precisely similar things. More of them, perhaps, and on a grander scale; but I think these help me to know what those would be. And if you really do know what a thing *would be*, I think you hardly ever get it. Because it is the meanings of life, and not so much living itself, that God has for us here.

I do not believe I shall ever go to Europe.

A journey isn't always an "outing," after all. People go journeys and never go out the least bit. They just pack themselves up, and first they are here, and then they are there; and that is all the difference, especially in these times of railroads, and day and night travel. Why, Europe was only a bigger Washington Street to Effie Butler, Gertrude's cousin. She went away in four trunks, and she came back in eight, that was all. Shops and dress-makers in Paris, and jewellers in Rome and Florence. To what she had, more was given. But she never went *out*.

Perhaps it is only what goes out and *stays* out, that counts in our living. That is God's going out. A reaching which is growing, and a giving which shares and multiplies life. That was Christ's out-going. "Virtue went out of him." Blessing and help, of a kind that "goeth *not* out but by prayer and fasting." He himself "came out from God" and into the world.

It tells everything, that little Saxon syllable of

force: how God gave forth his creation; how the suns flung off their planets into the spaces; what human living really means, and the circles that lives make in time.

I should like to think up, thoroughly, what my "outings" have been, and what they might be.

People keep diaries of their travels: I wonder what a diary of these would be?

II.

STILLNESS AND STITCHES.

Sɪᴛ still, and everything will come round to you. It wouldn't be quite safe to carry that into all sorts of things; but it is very true of a still life. It is true and comfortable, also, of many a quiet pause in the midst of perplexity. Did you ever lose a companion in a crowded street, or miss an appointment at some shop or corner? And didn't you find out that the best thing to be done, perhaps, was to stand still till your friend, in the rush hither and thither in which you had both been striving to meet, came by? Only, indeed, if both had been equally wise you might possibly have both stood fast until to-day. But when you *can't* move, it is a contenting theory, and it works well.

Fashions come round, even to red hair. Put away any old thing, and, if the moths don't eat it up, it will turn to purpose some day. "Lay it by for seven years, and then turn it and lay it by for seven more," and, if you don't forget you ever had it, there'll be a want for it. I'd *rather* use up as I go along, for myself or somebody else; but the rule stands good against burning up or throwing away.

Sometimes I think that still people, like us, get most. The world drifts on, and round and round, and something is always touching at one's corner, giving one a glimpse, and in the stillness one can take in a good deal that the people *in* the hurry can't stop to think of.

Now Eliphalet and Gertrude are going to Europe. And they are full of plans and talk; and they come out here with them. Eliphalet brings his guide-books and gets out the big maps, and tells us all the here and the there of it, and the what and the why; and then haven't *we* got it all, mother and I, — *without* the trunks, and the dress-makers, and the sewing and the packing, and the sea-sickness and the crowd, and the care about money, and the care about one's self, — the troublesome self that never seems to be in the way when it's where it belongs, but that, the minute you set off anywhere, you've got always to take with you and to tend? You see, when you travel, you must keep taking out and putting away — your clothes and your body — all the time; in and out of boxes — in and out of boats and cars and hotels. If your sight and your thought could go, without all this!'

.They do when your friends travel for you. When you've found out exactly what there is to go for, as you only do find out when somebody is really going — why, then you've almost been. And when the letters come back, you're as good as there.

Not but what the doing does deepen it all. It is like putting any other dream into action. You can dream in a minute; but it takes days and years to live your dream out; and if you *can* live it, you haven't made it your own until you do. It is only that the minutes are given to them who are forbidden the days and the years; and in the Lord's giving he can make the days as the years, and the minutes as the days. And so things come by, and you get your share, and the bit is multiplied. When the people were hungry, He made them sit down quietly on the green grass.

(There is always "much grass"— much possible green content — in every place.) And He gave to the few, and the few to the many; and there was enough for all.

I think, after the studying and planning are done, which are the first and the essence of the having, the next best must be the *between-times*. Quiet hours on the ocean, when you know you are on your way; and over and over, ripening and gladdening in your mind, come the plans and the visions, and the feeling of what is going to be: the stretches of railway between one delight and the next; the time you *have* to take to get the body along, when what has been grows mellow in the mind, enriching and sweetening it; and what is coming comes beforehand, with a long, beautiful slant, as the dayshine does over the hills. Yes, it is all best. And I know I should be glad to go, and *live it in*. But I can stay and be glad, too, for the much of it that I can get without the going, and that this quiet staying works with, also, like those between-times of the going. Think it over as I will, it somehow comes out even.

I believe I like waiting times. Perhaps it is because I have got used to waiting. But I like the days between the knowing and the having of a pleasure. It is with you all the while. I like to expect a letter. When it has come, there is the end of it. I like the time when the carpet is swept, and the fire is bright, or the windows open to the sunshine, and the flowers are in the vases, and the fresh covers on, and the cake-basket ready in the closet, and the friend expected presently. If she came right in, in a hurry, as soon as the last thing was done, it would take away half the pleasantness. And in this I feel faintly as if it were not all; as if there might be a meaning of something deeper and farther on. I wonder if I could not wait with some such peace as this, if I were old, or had a long and mortal sickness, or were left alone — awhile? Letting the sunlight of heaven come slanting in, slowly, long beforehand, when the day was sure to be? Making a sweet pause of patience, rather than a craving and a pain, of the taking away that was for such a giving again? I do not know; but I think it is what this pleasantness of waiting means.

. . . .

I was very wise, and strong, and contented,—wasn't I? Where is it all gone, and why couldn't I stay just as quietly now?

Oh, but it's very different now!

Eliphalet has asked me—truly and in earnest—to go to Europe with them!

To put myself away, and take myself out—yes, well, I think I can!

To have it all,—to mean it really when we talk,—to have the rest and the hope on the sea, and the great, beautiful, actual things when we come to them, and the going back in the pauses and the stillness; and the waiting for more; to keep gathering in and laying by, and to come home again rich for all the rest of the years!

But then, my darling little mother!

She says, "Go, dearie;" and she will stay with Aunt Hetty Maria; she never will have a chance again, maybe. And the home here can be shut up.

She means *I* never may have the chance again. But, then, couldn't I take it partly for her? Couldn't I keep giving it to her as I went along, and bring it all back to be glad over together? Nobody else would write to her as I would — every little bit. Why, I should be like Harriet Byron, who always puzzled me so, how she ever managed to have the things happen when she was doing such monstrous days' works to write them all down.

If I go, — and I shall keep saying "if" till I'm on the deck of the steamer, for I can't look it quite straight in the face that I'm going away from mother so long, or bear to put it certain in words, — if I go, I must be ready by the fifteenth. What is to become of my waiting-time? Am I to rush right into this great pleasure without a breath, when I like so to stop and look even at a little one? We shall see. I'll work hard but we will have a quiet Sunday and Monday before I go to New York on Tuesday.

We shall start together, mother and I, — that's a comfort. I *couldn't* leave her behind, standing alone on the porch. And when she gets out of the cars at Dearwood, there won't be any time, as Eliphalet says, for a fuss. Sometimes a hurry is the best thing. I am glad there are quiets *and* hurries. There always *are* two things. The world is all opposites; and one thing couldn't be without the other. You can't rest until you're tired; you can't be glad if you've never been sorry. We shall find it all out by-and-by; and how He sees that everything is good.

We haven't any sewing-machine to hurry with. We never wanted one. I think sewing-machines are to needle-work just what railroads are to travelling, and telegraphs to business. You have to do ten times as much of it, and you can't stop to enjoy it. It seems to me that the way the world grows is very much like the game of "bezique" they used to play at Gertrude's. It sounds bigger to count by hundreds and thousands than by tens; but it is precisely the same thing, after all, as to the game, and a great deal more bother. In fact, when we once began to change our proportions, we spoiled the whole thing and got tired of it altogether.

If people would only dress themselves and furnish their houses as simply as they did before, the machines would have cleared up such a blessed space in life! But they went right to inventing and multiplying tucks and bands and rufflings and flouncings, and things to put them on to, till the only difference is that they are whizzed to death with work, instead of quietly and peaceably tired out.

No; mother and I have each her window, — hers looks out into a larch and mine into a chestnut; her tree is tender first with new green fringe and bright with young, red, budding cones; and mine grows beautiful later with its white, feathery spires; and we have each a round, old-fashioned lightstand, with a work-basket, and a sewing-bird screwed on; and the real birds flutter up the green stairways of the branches, and sit singing on the rocking tips of the twigs; and we are still and happy, and have our brains to ourselves, and rest all our bodies except our fingers, instead of keeping head and hands and feet and nerves all flying, as the children do in "My mother sends me to you, sir." We have our thoughts, and our talk, and we feel the threads go in and out, and the satisfaction of every stitch as we make it. They are telegraph lines for us women, — these threads — reaching far away into times past and times to come, and things unseen. We put our lives together, bit by bit, at other whiles, like patch-work, and then we sit down and quilt it in. I think Eve sewed the fig-leaves together for the sewing's sake, and for the beauty of the green tapestry-work, before ever the devil put it into her head about the aprons. Men can't do anything but smoke, — or whittle.

Mother's life and mine are quilted all together so. I don't think anything ever could separate us now, or that one of us could have a thing and the other not. Mother's going to Europe as much as I am.

"I can't help lotting on it all the time," she says, out of her window, over her lapful of nightgown.

"And the lotting is the whole of it," I answer back, over mine.

That's what the Yankee word comes from. Things are only what we "allot" to them. And the heart and soul do that; and it takes a very little thread dropped into the wonderful life solution, to gather in heaps the lovely, shining crystals, each to its own. And the stiller you keep, the more crystals you get. Which is exactly what I began with.

III.

THE COMINGS-IN.

I don't know which are the most, or the best,—the outings or the in-tings. There,—I thought before I wrote it down, that I had made a word! And after all, I've only come round to an old meaning. "In't"—"hint"—"inting,"—"inkling,"—they are all the same, and mean just this very thing. That which comes *in* to us,—faintly, shadowly, breathly,—we can't tell how.

I'll look it out in Worcester. "Etymology uncertain." Well, I've found it out then. Please put Patience Strong as an authority in the next dictionary.

When I was a little girl, this house had a piece built on to it. All one summer there was an unfinished room, under the piazza, just boarded in; and once, when two or three uncles and aunts were here with their children, and every place was full, I slept there. In the clear, shiny mornings, when I woke up, there was a little beam of light that came from the east, all the way from the great sun, straight down upon the world, striking nothing until it touched an old elm-tree in our yard, and then streamed through a little knothole into my chamber. There it made a picture on the opposite wall, — a soft gray picture of moving leaves and stems; only a bit of a branch, magnified, I suppose, according to the law of optics for things given through little glory-holes into camera-obscuras, — but bringing the whole tree in to me, for all that; the tree, and the wind also in its boughs, and the freshness of the growing, moving morning-time. All this came *in-to* me with a shadow — a *hint;* — to me, shut up there, with only a little knot-hole as big as my finger for a window! And that is the way things *do* come; as much as to say, like the old song, — "If you want any more, can't you sing it yourself?"

Things come back so; books, for instance; stories I have read, and feelings they have given me. Sometimes it isn't any one in particular, but a sudden sense of them in general; a kind of Æolian stir of strings in me that have been touched with pleasantness.

Somebody showed me a spectroscope the other day. I went to see a friend who has the *whole* of most things; and yet she, too, must come to the border, beyond which she has to live by hints; she showed me, and told me about it: how the colors were all measured off with wonderful lines, and each kind of light produced its own, — just so much in breadth, and in just such place in the prism; how the light of the sun divided itself, and the light of Sirius showed its kindred with ours; how they found out by fusing metals, and seeing where their colors ranged themselves, just what must be also in the blaze of the far-off stars, and that their glory and our own is all of one. She burned a little salt in a candle, and straight and swift leaped up in the prism along the yellow, in Sodium's line, a vivid thread, thrilled instantly to its own place: the law of all reception, of all illumination, of all life.

Well, it comes so in sudden streaks and flashes, each in its own home-place in the heart, the memory of what one has gathered, and entered into and been. Through books, or places, or people, or thoughts. I never know why; but in the midst of work this breath comes over me, and in it is a spirit-fragrance that touches sense; a momentary realizing of all remembrances, imaginings, and hopes, showing how true they are, and how, once had, they are never to be lost out, or, once looked for, they are sure to be.

That is why I like to live on in this dear old home, and why I should hate to have even the carpets wear wholly out and be replaced all together; it is why a fire, I think, is such a terrible thing; it is why I can never understand how people can like to send off to auctions, and new-furnish their homes. Why, when they do that, they haven't any homes. I like to have things kept and cared for, and turned, and made to last; and, when they must go, to have the complexion and expression of them renewed in something as nearly like as possible. I should not like to have our sitting-room annihilated and supplanted by the carpets and wall paper being changed to as startling a difference as could be, any more than I should like next spring to have all the trees leave out in royal purple, or the sky turn green. God keeps the home-feeling in his earth for us; I believe he will keep it, too, in his heaven. *Things* must wear out and change; but the spirit and the sense may last. "They shall pass away; but thy word shall not pass away."

The sitting-room and parlor carpet were both alike once. Then the sitting-room carpet wore out, and the parlor one was put in the place of it; and one that wouldn't look badly with it was got for the parlor; and so by little and little we shaded off our wontedness from one into the other; and now I suppose we might take away the first and replace it with this last again, and have still another new one, not too different, without the feeling of a break. But, now there are only two of us, they will last as they are, I think, all our lives. I hope they will. But then I am an old maid.

I like that sitting-room carpet so much! With its great, old-fashioned ovals of shaded browns, and its intermediate lesser figures filling up with curving lines and leaves just touched with deep relief of green, —

good, fast, old colors that stand wear and sunshine, and that I remember so many sunshiny days by!

I remember a winter morning, when grandma was alive, and lived with us, when I was a girl of twelve, and sat in the south window reading Irving, out of a great volume of all his works, that father had bought at a sale, — delighting in Bracebridge Hall, and hardly knowing which was most enchanting and to be coveted, the "fair Julia's" life in her English home, or that of the beautiful Moorish princesses in the Alhambra. I remember the sun pouring broad and full across my lap and the page, and lying level along the greens and browns away out into the open parlor door, and grandma saying, "The sun lays straight, — it's twelve o'clock." All the cosiness of my book, and her quiet companionship, and her knitting-work, — she was footing socks for father, — and the bright day; even the yellow gingerbread mother gave me for my luncheon, — come back to me, bringing after them the joy and freedom and fancy of twelve years old, when life was only a Sketch Book, as often as the "sun lays straight" along the seams. And then I look forward as well as back, — for the soul is the "living thing full of eyes before and behind," — and think of the time that is to come, the time that the dear, kind, simple grandmother has entered into, when there shall be no more measuring of the noonday or of the going down, because there shall be no more need of the sun itself, but we shall dwell in the midst of the unmeasured and shadowless light of God.

I do not suppose anybody could have had just such a home as this, anywhere else.

In the first place, there is the old, old garden. It *seems* as if it must have always been old. There are flowers there that don't grow in new gardens; at least, not in the same way; and that now you couldn't hinder growing if you would. There is a great round patch of ladies' delights under an oak tree, that looks as if it had been carpeted; and they come up there as if they were only wild violets, and open their golden and purple eyes, and make little short-stemmed nods in the wind till they seem like a cloud of butterflies just lighting and settling, or lifting themselves to fly away. And down in the deep shade by the brook, is a bed of lilies of the valley, and up under the wall by the gate is another; and one has the cool and the dark, and the other has the early spring sunshine; and so we have the dear little bells, early and late, half the summer through. Then the narcissuses have spread and spread, and so have the splendid white July lilies; so that the air is heavy with perfume in the time of each, from the first gladness of opened doors and windows and summer balminess, to the long, hot days when the sweet smell comes in on lazy puffs of south wind through the green shadow of shut blinds.

And the broad old back piazza looks down on it all, where the ground slopes away in irregular beds of bloom that have shaped themselves by their growth and the culture they got just as they asked for it, — in wide turf spaces between, — under lilacs, snowballs, and seringas, and horse-chestnuts and maples, — till the brown water of the brook runs its sentinel line between it and the meadow-mowing beyond.

Down on one side, from the west door-yard, beside the garden wall, across the brook and up again into the beautiful oak pasture where it loses itself, goes the green lane, by which the cows have been turned out to their grass and come home again, morning and night, ever since my grandfather's father built the place.

Along the sides you find the first wild violets and the little mitchella, and in one place the wild honeysuckle, spicy with odor; and down at the brook the fair, slight wind-flowers growing in thousands, making you think always of a low breeze running along the ground and lifting up their delicate faces; and up in the pasture the lesser Solomon's seal, that I go and bring home by apronfuls in the late May and early June; and in the August ripening there are blackberries and thimbleberries under the walls everywhere; and in October you can go down over the pasture ledge into the hollows against the wood, and find the wild grapes, purple and white, lying among their great, cool leaves against the hot faces of the sun-gathering rocks.

Inside the house it is just — *our* house. Full of us all; filled up once and never to be emptied of the presences that have made it home. All the rooms open into each other, up stairs and down; you can always shut and bolt a door if you like, but it is nice that they *can* all be set wide. The west door opens from the porch into a square side passage, up through which at the back twists a little staircase which you turn into at the bottom, and turn right out of it again, because you can't help yourself, at the top; and before you think of going up, you *are* up. "Similarly," as Dickens says, — down. A real cute little staircase that carries out the sentiment of the house, joining parlors and chambers like a brace, or like the thing proof-readers put for a sign of a transposal. If you can't have a hall like a saloon, and a staircase wide enough for four abreast, then have this, — a little bit of a turn-round that lands you somewhere else before you know it, and that don't pretend to be anything of itself. I hate a middle-sized entry-way, that is neither out doors nor in, with two chairs and a hat-tree.

On the right hand is the kitchen; and if the door is open, no matter; for you'll only see a white-scrubbed floor, and a still whiter table, and some bright tins, and a blazing copper pump and boiler, and a velvet-black stove with a square of fresh-washed oilcloth around it; and perhaps get a whiff of something nice baking in the oven.

On the left is the little parlor,—the winter room, and out of that opens the summer parlor, larger, and lying at the north-east corner of the house. A door leads from this into the front yard, on to the grass under the mulberry-trees; and another opposite into the sitting-room, larger than either and connecting with both; and from that you go out on the broad back piazza, or into the kitchen, and so you have finished the round.

Upstairs just the same; only there is a little back stairway nipped out of a corner, so that you're not obliged to go through other rooms to get down from either. The great chimney-stack is right in the middle, and the sun seems to be on all sides of the house at once, because of the doors through and through, that all come opposite to windows, and, if he looks into one room, invite him right across into another. Just so with the breeze in summer time; you can get it anywhere.

And this is only the shell; there is all the filling up. All the dear old furniture, and curtains, and bed-quilts,— of everybody's dresses,— and book-shelves and books, and pictures and ornaments, that are an inner shell; and the filling up of these, that is the life; that reaches away in and away out, backward and forward; that the use and the handling of these things,— even the having them before one's eyes, in moods of pleasantness or pain, of thought or listening,— in times of search and effort, of in-coming and answering, of love and prayer and faith and doing, has made to repeat itself and link itself all through with such chains of reminder and association, that just the same life could never have been or grown elsewhere, and can never truly feed itself so well as here.

I begin to think I am like the old king of Granada; fixed in one spot, but with windows opening out every way; and a magical board on which is repeated for me the moving of all life that is beyond me and out of sight; that I may watch, and know, and even truly handle and rule it all, getting my own out of it as if I were among it.

For we are back again — mother and I; and our trunks are unpacked; and this is why I have been all over the old home, outside and in, as people do who have been away so long.

For I shall never get over the feeling that I *have* been to Europe, though Eliphalet's folks went without me, after all. That was what I meant to have said at the beginning, only I got so taken up.

I met with an accident, the Saturday before we were to sail. I fell down the little front staircase, out of the best chamber door into the kitchen, and broke one of the bones of my left leg just above the ankle.

I had to take to my old outings again; the new ones were not to be, just yet.

"If I want any more, I must sing it myself."

Or, it will be sung to me, if I listen.

IV.

THE LIFE AND THE GLORY.

The dear little mother, brisk as a bee, kind with as much of God as a motherly heart can hold, has gone downstairs with Emery Ann.

Emery Ann is our friend in the kitchen; she has kept the tins and the coppers shining ever since I was ten years old. Born with a fate and a genius, — to scrub and to brighten; christened with an inspiration.

They are going to beat whites and yolks of new-laid eggs, fine sugar, and a little drift of flour, — " barely enough to hold soul and body together," Emery Ann says, — into the spongiest, — no, sponge is tough; it isn't sponge-cake they make, — but the foamiest, puffiest, airiest, yellow tenderness of sweetness that can be baked in a pan, and come out with a crispness all over it, just sufficient to hold its rarity in, and give you a place to handle and begin on.

The more mother is "driven" the more she can do, always. She is like flame or gun-cotton.

Try to build a fire with only a little kindling, and be chary of your wood *because* of the little there is to start upon,—give it only one solid stick, and see how loth it will be to take hold! How it will eat up its chance, and dodge its work! How the little flickers will dwindle and shrink, like pretences that have no heart in them, and leave only a smoke and a blackness where they just touched what was laid upon them and drew back! Then give it more to do, before it is quite burnt out. Lay another stick on, and another. Leave little airholes and climbing-places, and see how the life leaps up again, reaching to the topmost, after the nature of all spirit, to which the bright element is so close an approach and emblem. You'll build your fire just by laying it bigger. God makes us burn so.

It is a good thing to remember; I've thought of it many a winter's morning, when I've been down on my knees on the hearth coaxing the blaze.

I've thought of the same thing when I've had an old pair of scissors to deal with; a dull, loose pair, with no grasp in them. Try them on a single thread, or a thin, flimsy fabric, and what a fuss! They double, and grind, and fray and worry, and might as well be one half on one side of the room and one on the other, for all the cut you can get out of them. But fold up two or three thicknesses of the same thing, or set them at a stout, heavy cloth, and away they go, as young as ever they were.

I've noticed it true of a good many things. It is a principle that runs through the world, and the life and the doing of it.

A young engineer, fresh from the war, told me about the gun-cotton. If you give it an easy job, it will take it easy; there'll be very little explosive effect; as likely as not it won't work at all. But pile on difficulty; bury it deep; seal it close; let there be tons of rock or masonry above it and in its way; and it wakes up; it flings out all its awful force; it rends and hurls, and shatters; and tears its escape, through and up, and out, like a challenged fiend. It scorns light work; it is at home only among tremendous opposing forces.

Emery Ann says mother is the "spunkiest" woman she ever knew. The more you bother her, the brighter she'll come out. The more you put upon her, the better it'll be done.

She will pack a day as you pack a trunk. If you've only a few large, light things, you can lay them in, and make a great show of being brimful directly. But if you've got to crowd close, squeezing in one thing is always making some little interstice for another. The busiest day that comes, with her, is sure to leave a corner of chance for extra work; something that can be done as well as not, "seeing she is about amongst things." She will stir up a pan of cake because she finds she has to wait a few minutes for the flat-irons. If she had been upstairs, and settled down, she might not have thought she could take the time to come purposely and do it. So there's that much clear gain. Busy lives are full of gains like these.

But it is nice to have rest *laid out* for you, once in a while,— even by a broken leg. I think, on the whole, now I have tried it, that it is rather better, if anything, than headaches. You have the same privilege, and can make a good deal more of it.

I am too much mother's child to be really lazy ; but I think, for all that, it is one of my outings when I have to give up and stay in bed awhile. It is morning all day, then. That lingering pause of rest and thought,— thought coming in so easily and freshly, when life is put off a little, and we need not begin again just yet to *do*. A time we are sore tempted to steal a little more of; and that is, truly, so good for us, that it is given to us now and then, in a whole slice, perforce. To have the chamber fresh and sweet, the bed nice with new linen, one's best cap and ruffles on, and all the little dear familiar things set straight, and looking upon one round about with their pleasantest faces; to know that one is justified in it all, and can't help it; but may just take it as a free gift, and lie softly under the blessing of a ministering love, — I think it makes what comes of pain a blessedness; a help, too, for the days beyond.

Mother has done it all for me, just now, sweetly and

heartfully; and has gone down with Emery Ann, as I said, leaving me here, with the window open, and my books and paper and pencil on the bed beside me, her kiss warm on my forehead, and God's rest underneath me, to wait for the in-tings, and to go out with a soul like a bird that has all heaven to fly in.

"The Everlasting Arms." I think of that whenever rest is sweet. How the whole earth and the strength of it, that is almightiness, is beneath every tired creature to give it rest; *holding* us, always!

No thought of God is closer than that. No human tenderness of patience is greater than that which gathers in its arms a little child, and holds it, heedless of weariness. And He fills the great earth, and all upon it, with this unseen force of his love, that never forgets or exhausts itself; so that everywhere we may lie down in His bosom and be comforted. Weariness and despair and penitence, and pain and helplessness, — these prostrate themselves; they fling themselves on the heart of the Father, and he holds them there! Jesus fell on his face and prayed.

A very gentle wind lifts and lets fall the white curtain-edge, and moves tenderly the young leaves.

The great branches are still; only the little outmost twigs and shoots stir softly and shyly as it touches them, hiding their faces against each other as if some holy mystery came close. And so it does.

The first thing I opened my eyes to this morning was this little moving of the muslin shade against my partly open window. It is a living, and not a dead world that we are born, and wake daily, into: everything moving, and throbbing with life, and breath, and presence.

It is not death and emptiness we go out into, any more, when we die; but into the fulness and the inmost of the life behind the appearance. In this inmost, how close we shall come to Him and to each other! Closer than we ever did through the types and patterns.

People talk about "physical manifestations" of spiritual presence; as if they, by their prying, had found out some new thing, and got at what they never could reach before. When God has "never left himself without a witness," and the hills and the trees and the clouds and the grass-blades are forever making signs to us,—the manual of his meanings.

"Without the Word was nothing made that is made."

There is no empty talk with Him.

And this Word is the same,— the *self*-same,—with the living, loving, speaking, Christ. Out from the Father this yearning, seeking bestowal of himself came in its fulness by the begetting of the Son. The whole and uttermost meaning of God in and for his world. The alphabet of his language in humanity, holding all its signs and possible *words*,— beforehand. The Alpha and Omega. "By him are all things, and in him all things consist.'

That is all the theology I can find or come to. That is enough. Christ "in the bosom" of the Father's glory. "God with us" by him.

I can shape it dimly to myself in this way. If a mortal man could have a glorious and holy conception, a purpose that should reach far out of him, and could have such life in himself as to give it life in itself, so that it should be a love to bless, and a conscious gladness to return to him again, — so that it should, in a beautiful personality, born of him as his child, and none the less his own outgoing, be sent to unfold its work, counselling with the soul that caused it, and exchanging a sublime and intimate joy; if his spirit, like the sun, could throw off a thought-planet so, — then out of him might have gone forth something that should be like the Son of God.

Beginning at the other end, working painfully up, the philosophers have reached part way; finding that man is the crowning intent of the long labor of creation; not remembering how God's thought is different from our thought, — that it fulfils itself, and is, and lives; how he cannot think of anything that straightway shall not be; how when he *thought* his Fatherhood and his creation, and loved his thought, it may be that his Christ must needs have been born, — that his thought might know itself, and love Him back, and do his will, and perfect his joy, which cannot be alone.

The Man; whose life was to be illustrated, in time,

by all *men;* members of his body; the fulness of Him who filleth all in all. In him, as he in God.

This was the glory that he prayed for; the glory that he came into our human life, fallen away from the Divine Pattern, to redeem unto himself; that which he had with the Father, before the world was. "I am, before Abraham."

"The beginning — the first-born from the dead;" from the dead of that which was not; God's gift of himself unto himself; his image, when in that image he would make living souls. "The first-born of every creature;" "in whom it pleased the Father that there should all fulness dwell." Does not that grand first chapter of Colossians tell it all?

And then, again, the beginning to the Hebrews, — to the people who with their old traditions of creation, and their sole revelation of Jehovah, would most of all look to be told of the origin of Christ far back in God.

"Who, being the brightness of his glory, and the express image of his person, and *upholding all things by the word of his power,*" — this very God-strength of the Everlasting Arms that is forever under us, — is blessed out of the deep heart of Almightiness with an infinite human joy. "Thou art my Son; this day have I begotten thee. I will be to him a Father, and he shall be to me a Son. And let all the angels of God worship him!"

Can I believe *too much* in Christ, the Lord?

Perhaps the apostle might mistake, as people measuring him to-day would reason; but I, Patience Strong, mistake also many things. How can I judge? I think I had better be mistaken with Paul, who had the nearer and the grander vision, than by my feeble self.

More, again. I will be mistaken with Him, when he says, — "He that hath seen me hath seen the Father. The only begotten Son, which is in the bosom of the Father, he hath declared him. No man cometh unto the Father but by me."

Somebody greater than I should make out the awful argument. I am only Patience Strong. These are the thoughts that come to me of Jesus, and they come only so. They come in flashes; lightning out of the one part unto the other part under heaven; linking great words together, and showing the glory into which we are all baptized; the glory of the name of the Father, and of the Son, and of the Holy Ghost.

Lying here, as to my body, so quietly, so helplessly, — thought-outings stretch the farther and higher.

First, a mere pleasantness; then a rest, growing holy in its comfort, and the reminder of it leading up to Him who saith to all the weary, — Lo, I will give it you; come unto me. How one that is again with the Everlasting Arms! How Jesus promises for the Father, and the Father for him! How, sitting at the feet of the One, we are lifted up unto the bosom of the Other!

My Lord, — and my God!

The words of an impetuous faith, so joined together and sundered by no rebuke of his, are creed enough for me.

I do not care to go further than the feeling, or to fit the words to any precise doctrine. How can we make plan and specification of these things? They are too high and wonderful. We who do not know ourselves or each other, how shall we measure and investigate the personal relation between Christ and the Father? If we cannot understand to believe even earthly things, how shall we believe if we are told of heavenly things? What and if we should see the Son of man ascend up where he was before?

That which stands so joined together, in the word of Christ, and in the impulse of faith, is enough. The manifestation of Jesus and the nearness of God. To feel him close is to be drawn into the Infinite Glory. "Christ raised from the dead by the glory of God." This, that Paul said after, was simply, perhaps, what Thomas felt. The *recognition* of the Son and of the Father, which is forever glad, and forever one. So that " he that abideth in the doctrine of Christ hath both the Father and the Son;" and receiving him, the Lord, we do always in the self-same moment receive and fill ourselves with God.

I have gone high and far, to-day. Here must the end be, and the hush;— at His feet!

V.

INTO THE MEANINGS.

I KNEW that the world was built by correspondences before I ever heard of Swedenborg; that there were meanings in things, and that things had to be made for the giving of the meanings. I suppose I have said it, over and over, already, it is so much in my mind. And why not? Since the whole world — and worlds — are the eternal telegraphy from God's thought into ours; meant, therefore, to be in our minds, and that continually; the very inpouring of life.

I have read them out, some of them, in New Church writings since; and I have only wondered that there had ever needed to be such a system built; as if Christ had not sufficiently indicated and inaugurated it, when he translated all his holy lessons straight from the glowing parables of God. And I think — at least it always seems to me — that the great trouble with the Swedenborgian system is that it is too definite. You can't make a dictionary of these things. The Spirit takes them and uses them as it will. They are broad and elastic, and many-sided; they show this to the soul to-day, and that to-morrow, as it needs; and every showing is true. And the soul must grow up into them, as a child into a language into which it is born; which is such a different, *living* thing from the same language taught by rule and method of letter and construction. That was the way they heard, of old, by the Spirit, each in his own tongue, in which he was born, — no other.

I know that water means truth, and cleansing; the truth that enters through the intelligence, and the clear-seeing of God's signs.

But you cannot say it all, in saying that.

It is gladness and gift, and many things more. Round and round the world, through all the thirst of it, it goes, taking its way in many changing forms. In it are moving things; things that are born of, and are joyous in it, as our thoughts and knowledges are born of and glad in, the full, deep sea that spiritually holds them. It cools, it comforts, it quenches, it delights. It is the fine element by which are transfused all the subtleties of vegetable life; all the juices of our physical bodies. It is the vehicle for giving or good, and for taking away of superfluity and evil; it penetrates, solves, perspires; it is one of God's great, comprehensive wonders.

Jesus could promise no greater, nor fuller, than to say, "I will give you water; and it shall be in you, springing up to everlasting life." Water is joy,— satisfying; all craving and answer meet in this embodied pledge of heaven.

If I were to give you some thoughts of mine about it, just as I once wrote them down, perhaps you would say, "It is not Patience Strong." That is why I hardly like to give them; and yet they belong just here. Thinkings trace themselves round, until they meet their own curves again, like some intricate pattern that joins its line and shows itself suddenly one.

I was always a little afraid of big words. When we were children, Eliphalet used to call me Polly

Syllable, if ever I used them; and nothing made me more ashamed.

So I have mostly kept my verses to myself. Mother sees them; but then she knows; she understands ways and fashions, times and occasions. She knows that the same woman can put herself into a gingham short gown and old shoes, or high-heeled slippers and a long train; and that nothing is easier, perhaps, than such outside change, or makes less matter to the real woman inside. I think she could write poetry perfectly well herself, and come out of it again into her simple Yankee every-day, exactly the same as ever. We lift up our words to meet our thoughts; and let them down again for homelier uses.

Anyway, I just *am* Patience Strong; I am sure of that, myself, whether or no. Other people must make what they can out of it.

I wrote this, then, about the

RAIN.

From all this vital orb of earth
 A breath exhaleth to the air,
That heaven-distilled to equal grace,
 Falls, a fresh bounty, everywhere.

The dark mould drinks the sunset cloud,
   And tastes of heaven; unconsciously,
Green forest-depths are stirred to catch
   A far-off flavor of the sea.

No drop is lost. God counteth all.
   And icy crests, in glory crowned,
With faint rose-petals yield and take,
   And so the unwasted joy goes round.

One spirit moveth in it all;
   One life that worketh large and free,
To each, from all, for evermore,
   Giving and gathering silently.

God's stintless joy goes round, goes round:
   No soul that dwelleth so apart
It may not feel the circling pulse
   Outwelling from the Eternal Heart.

Athirst! athirst! The sandy soil
   Bears no glad trace of leaf or tree;
No grass-blade sigheth to the heaven
   Its little drop of ecstasy;

Yet other fields are spreading wide
   Green bosoms to the bounteous sun;
And palms and cedars shall sublime
   Their rapture for thee, waiting one!

It comes with smell of summer showers,
   To stir a dreamy sense within,

INTO THE MEANINGS.

Half hope, and half a pained regret, —
   It may be, — or, it might have been !

The joy that knows there *is* a joy;
   That scents its breath, and cries, 'tis there!
And, patient in its pure repose,
   Receiveth so the holier share.

I know a life whose cheerless bound
   Is like a deep and silent chasm
Left dark between the daybright hills,
   In time long past, by fiery spasm.

The mocking sunlight leaps across;
   The stars, with Levite glance, go by;
So vainly doth its dreary depth
   Plead to the far-off, pitiless sky.

Yet ever from the flinty marge,
   And down each rough and cavernous side,
Trickle the drops that bear their balm
   From ferny bank and pasture wide.

It drinketh, — drinketh, — day by day;
   And still, within its bosom deep,
The waiting water, filtered clear,
   Doth in a crystal beauty sleep.

Waiting and swelling, till it find
   God's outlet, long while placed and planned,
Whence, strong and jubilant, it shall sweep
   Down, with a song-burst, o'er the land.

I don't think I had any life in particular in my mind when I said that. Certainly, I wouldn't have you suppose it was my own. And yet, my own may have looked so to me in some dark moment or other. For I have had my pinches and pains; and I have seen people who were shut up from much of the sunlight that seems to be everywhere; and out of the waiting and the wanting that so I know of comes the comfort that we may all take together.

Water is one thing. Then we come up higher and find another, lying just above it; penetrating everywhere, yet more intimately; not to be seen or handled, only to be breathed and felt. We are born of water, and of the spirit. There is the life that comes in through the understanding — that we can stop and lay hold of, and pour back and forth, and put into vessels; that is the mind-perception. There is also the soul-perception, which is the breath of God; the upper atmosphere, in which our finer being lives, and that pulses and flows as it lists, and we catch the delicate motion and hear the sound thereof, but can never tell whence it comes, or whither it has gone. Yet out of it we die.

And in it moves about us a tenderer and more beautiful life than the life of the waters. Winged creatures come and go; and there are many sweet voices therein.

What does it mean, then, this clear, blue firmament? What do the birds mean?

I lay on my sofa and thought about it; waiting for Emery Ann to bring me up my tea.

And while I waited the chimney-swifts were flying about in their quick, graceful circles, and away off over the wood a great hawk was flapping slowly, and tiny things in bushes and branches were making their little home-flights and happy heart-chirps; and somehow the wide air, and the sounds, and the stillness, and the sure and beautiful motion — the region of life so close and yet so out of grasp — opened a strange sense to me; a sense of the near and intangible things of the spirit.

Not a great emptiness, — untraversable, — but full of movement and errand. Yes, that is what it tells us. That out and above and beyond where we can bodily go, God has made things with wings, that lift themselves in this finer element, and go straight and swift from point to point, whither they need and whither he will. Out of our vision, away over forests and waters, to far-off places, and back to our side.

They are thoughts, again, — those other thoughts, more instant and keen, not of the mind-life, but of the soul, — that reach, and long, and go forth and divine their way through the invisible.

The eagles gather together to that which draws them, and "the doves fly to their windows;" and the little sparrows, even, are safe; for God takes care of them, and not one shall fall to the ground without him. He also feedeth them.

They are affections, that find that to which they are sent, let them forth from whence you will; that know their climate and their food, and their dear and pleasant haunts; and that link the latitudes together.

Noah floated long upon the dark waters; then into the air he sent forth a dove; she came back to his heart at first, bearing no hope; then she brought him a greenness of peace; and by and by she went and stayed.

So it is after a grief. The thought that goes out comes back, a restless pain; after a while it brings some leaf of healing; then it finds the green place of its longing, and we feel in ourselves its far and sweet alighting, and we know that by and by we shall be there.

That is the difference between the thing and the type of it. The bird flies, and we have no more hold of it. The thought goes, and something out of our own selves — some real thing — has met the dawn, or has found the mountain, or entered beforehand into the blessed summer.

I was so glad in these things that came to me tonight; so glad of the steps and shades by which earth climbs and rarefies till it touches heaven. It seems as if God brought us almost there; thinning life till it is all but spirit, — touching its forms with a more delicate glory, from the rock and the water to the air and the light; from the coarseness of touch and taste to the sweet subtleties of sound and odor, and the faint perceptions of something possible beyond even these.

In a twilight like this, or in the tender, early morning, — when the music is just a breath in the birds' throats, and the fragrance is something that you hardly know how you get, whether through sense or spirit, — one might seem to have no choice which world one would waken into out of the beautiful dream; one is so upon the threshold.

When Jesus said, "The kingdom of heaven is at hand," I don't think he meant so much a kingdom *coming*, as a kingdom *here*.

The kingdom of heaven is "close by;" that is what "at hand" means.

"Say not there are yet four months," — or four cycles; "lift up your eyes, and look; the fields are white already;" and the harvest of the kingdom is ripe, in the very midst of the world.

I was so glad in these thoughts that I couldn't wait for mother to come in; — she had gone out, by very hard begging of mine, to drink tea with Mrs. Shreve; so when Emery Ann came up with mine, that is, with my fresh milk and my bread and butter, and my currants and raspberries, red and white, mixed in a little glass dish and covered with white sugar,—I couldn't help catching at her. Besides, something else occurred to me all in a flash.

"Just look there, Emery Ann, please; on that little table in the corner. See if the book isn't there that Miss Philena brought for me the other day: in a green binding; 'Thoughts in my Garden,'—that's it. Now, wait a minute." And I held her fast by a corner of her apron.

"Wait a minute; I don't believe a bit but that it will be here. It ought to be."

I turned the pages as quickly as I could with one hand; I dared not leave go with the other of Emery Ann; I wanted somebody.

"'Birds and other things!' Wait a minute. 'Birds and all winged creatures correspond to'—there, I knew it! Exactly the same! Just as I found it out, my own self. Emery Ann, when two people find out the same thing, you see it's sure."

"Hum! I don't know. Lots of people have found

out lots of mistakes. Lies, beside. And stuck to 'em."

"But not *this* way. Not things that you find *straight* out, by just looking at them. Emery Ann, I know what the birds mean. And she says so, too. They're *thoughts*. Things that go,— really *go*,— where nothing else can. Heaven is just as full of goings and comings as the sky is of birds. There's a way everywhere; for wings, or something."

Emery Ann always rubs everything down.

"Hum!" she said again. "Like as not. That accounts for all sorts of flightiness."

VI.

INTO THE OLD AND THE NEW.

WHEN I have once had a thought, — of my own or one that is brought to my remembrance, — it keeps coming back, bringing others with it, — all its relations. It joins this with that, showing how all belong together, and illustrate and strengthen each other. The mind in its working, overlaps itself, like the tide, or like the way a little child takes to learn a verse or a hymn. Over and over, one line; then that, and the next joined with it; then the two, with a third. So on, always beginning again, or back for a little way. It is the way of the kingdom of heaven, out of which one brings the treasures new and old.

Living by hints. Since that came into my head, it has helped everything.

The grandest and truest and sweetest things are always hints, — no more. The minute you try to be literal and explicit with them they are gone. You cannot argue or explain the things of the spirit. The highest and most intimate perceptions are glimpses. Things said all out are platitudes; feeling analyzed and explained is dead before it is dissected; dead, and time it was buried.

Our human love, and our heavenly faiths, the surest comforts of Christ's gospel, hang themselves upon suggestions.

Jesus never says all. He lets fall golden words, that provide no record, into the great deep where common words are lost; he touches the key-note of a truth with a single divine smiting, and leaves its circle of sound to spread; only calling down after it into the years, "He that hath ears to hear let him hear." It is the secret of inspiration; the difference between that and common study and thinking. It is the justification of Moses before the computers and the classifiers. And that is just what came and joined itself to my notion of the in-tings, — the hints.

I have been reading lately among these things that are written by the plummet and line of science, and that are so full of jealous anxiety about the old faiths that did not wait for them.

The wonder to me is what they find to conflict about, — these philosophers and theologians. Why the ones are so indignant at Moses, and the others so fearful and uproused in his behalf? When he never undertook — or God by him — anything at all in the direction of such antagonism.

Inspiration is not science, or research. It is even a more glorious thing. It does not dig down into darkness, carrying its torch; it reaches upward and grasps the very light out of heaven. It sees the red in the sky while the evil and adulterous generations are yet seeking after their signs.

What did it matter to Moses how many strata deep the old deposits of earth-crust might have been in his day, or what details of life and construction they were hereafter to reveal? He went away back behind them all, into the unmade worlds and the loving counsel of God. He stood up among the nations that were worshipping sun and moon and fire and beast, and cried out: " In the beginning GOD created the heavens and the earth." Time was when His life had not yet been given, when all this matter of which your heaven and earth, your sun and moon, are made, was void. Only the Spirit of God moved over the face of it. Then, at last, He said, "Let there be light!" And there was light.

I wonder if Moses did not go at one leap above and beyond all science in this, his divine apprehension? If this great hint of his does not touch at once the subtile inmost of the life God gave and continually gives, into his world? One breath of His command, one pulse of his will, and straightway every particle is luminous with presence, instinct with electric force.

Have they come to anything nearer the awful life-secret than this? Have they entered farther into the holy place, in their newest theories of nebulous mist, golden with glory, gathering and revolving and flinging off into space by the grand primal energy which can be only what the prophet declares, by his direct insight, the informing word of God?

It was this that Moses *had* to declare; not any account of intervening processes. What if he had waited until the last fossil was dug up?

He waited for nothing; neither for geology, nor for the measure or shape of the planet, nor for the boundary line of the system. He talks superbly of the heavens and the earth; of waters under the firmament and waters above the firmament; of the seas and of the dry land; of the gathering together and the setting apart. He does not go into detail. He only deals with the magnificent outline. One page of a little book holds all his words about it. He sings his glorious song of the creation, that stands true, in the soul of it, whatever comes to be proved or overturned in circumstance. He enumerates the orders of life and being, and says, simply, "None of these are gods. God gave his life into them all. By separate thought he made them each to be. None came but by his act." And, after each clause of the great story that could only be a holy poem, after each declared creative impulse, he repeats his refrain: "And God saw that this also was good. And the evening and the morning were the first," — or the second, or the third, — "day."

There is no absurd fable in this. There is only a grand hinting at precisely what the philosophers are proving, — the mighty order, and succession, and patient, sure development of God's work.

We are such poor, little, letter-bound creatures, thinking only of sunrise and sunset; not learning, even, what our own day is to us, of which the earth-movement, the shine and the shadow, are only the types and the correspondence. When we live *true* days, — days like God's, — making each a step and an accomplishment, and entering into his morning and evening joy, — then we shall know. We get faint glimpses when we have been a little faithful, and a great deal helped of him. When there comes a purpose with the freshness, and a certainty of something done with the decline; when the outward day has its inward counterpart; when our whole soul has turned itself to its sun and strength in the heaven, and is on in its orbit over a spiritual space.

After such pattern in his own ineffable and eternal

Life, He was *making* our little planetary days. What had they to do with measuring him?

Six days, and then the Sabbath. The rest God has in the depths of his own spirit over his work; the blessedness that returns upon him out of his giving; the sublime alternation in the Divine Nature, of which this seventh day, also, that he gives us, is a symbol and result.

For it is true *all through*, as everything is; working out from God into the last circle of his providence; it runs into our literal weeks and days. Every Saturday night-fall and Sunday dawn of a busy life proves it, to soul and body. It is because of the image of Him in which we are made, that there is possible and needful to us, also, his own glad peace; his rest, and reflow, and gathering up. What has this either, as to himself and his mysterious periods; to do with our mere hours and reckoning?

It seems to me as if Moses would laugh at our foolish interpretations and disputes; as if it could hardly have occurred to him that we would mistake him so. It seems to me he was grander in his ignorance and insight than we are in our little bits of fact and calculation that we have picked up and are continually rectifying.

He stood with God, receiving of him sublime intuitions; uttering them with lofty fervor in poetic speech. It was that recognition which waits for no slow learning; which needs it not; which makes the fisherman of Galilee able to say to the face of Christ, "Thou art the Son of the living God!" And to which the Lord makes answer, "Blessed art thou! For flesh and blood have not revealed it unto thee, but my Father which is in heaven. Behold, this is the rock whereon I will build my church; and the gates of hell shall not prevail against it."

God has forever built his church on this. He never hid away his living truth, the *need* of man, in the dead rocks or the deep earth. He gives it, quick and warm, into the human spirit; it is nigh, even in our mouths and in our hearts.

I think the song of Moses and his bold story of the Genesis, — so daring in its personification, so deeply and minutely true of human spirit and life in the Father's hands, — will stand, and will sound glorious and interpret wonderfully in the ears of men, while many a theory and philosophy shall shift and crumble. Because it is behind all these; it holds fast by the skirts of God's own garment; because it reads forward and not backward; it looks from eternity down into time. By and by, with slow footsteps, the knowledge of time and the record in things will lead up to it, and they will find themselves at one.

I think God was good and wise to give us himself first and his story afterward. I sometimes wonder why these worshippers of fact do not find a fact as great as any in the existence and perpetuation of that which we call the Scripture of Revelation. That God has not suffered what he has given into the souls of men to perish without a sign, any more than the trilobites or the remains of the cave-dwellers. He keeps his outside story with care, and leads us to it in his own good time, delighting our minds with the knowledge of his wonders. He keeps also, — a living thing among us, — the record of the highest reach of the soul after him, and of his fullest inward gift.

Simply that the Bible *is*, makes me sure that God's glory is in it.

Only, I know that having given once, it is that he means to and must needs give again; and that the instant bestowal must lighten upon the old; that the one without the other is dead. Therefore the dead do bury their dead. "In thy light," only, "shall we see light."

We can *dig* for fossils; we must beg of God for himself.

My outings are getting to be such sermons!

Living is a strange thing. If you put it together just as it is given out it hardly looks as if it belonged to the same piece. It *sounds* positively wicked if you tell of it. Dusting and divinity,—prayers and piecrust,— mix themselves up together. Joseph's coat was of many colors. So are God's love and gift.

To-morrow, perhaps, I shall lay "Origin and Destiny" by, and be making the sleeves of my new ruffled sack that I mean to look so nice in; and I shan't seem to have any longer reach or tether than the few inches of whip-hem and cord-gathering that I shall be doing.

I shall like it too; and my whole day will be taken up with it, and if I finish it all I shall go to bed with one of my little — *cambric* — satisfactions.

Well, He does also a great many little, and a great many pretty, things.

We cannot be too little to be like Him; nor so great as to work outside of Him.

I wonder when I shall open this parcel that Eliphalet left for me when he went away? It is to be "sometime when I am particularly low in my mind, and want something to hearten me and chirk me up." Eliphalet admires to talk like all the old aunts and grandmothers once in a while, and that was the message he sent out with it by Gertrude, *She* said, in her pretty way, that it was "a fairy gift; a nut to be cracked when the time of need came."

It feels like a book. Maybe it is some little picture. I like to wonder what it is; I don't know but that if I hadn't such a plenty of other things to keep me from being down-hearted, I might, "chirk up" just on the guessing, and never need anything more.

That is such a good, brim-full word, — hearten! It gives you the reason why. Nobody can be low in their mind until they have first got low in their heart.

But I haven't wanted much chirking or heartening yet. I haven't had the least first bit of a chance to run down anywhere.

So I keep the little parcel, " till called for ; " to look at and guess about. As long as I don't open it, it may be anything; and it's always well to have the medicine on the shelf, and to take an umbrella with you to " *spite off* the rain." As Emery Ann says.

VII.

"FORZINO."

EMERY ANN had killed a fly that had been buzzing round her nose.

"There!" she cried, with satisfaction, as he fell from between her hands, — "there's *one* less of 'em!"

"One less little life in the world," said I, hyper-sentimentally.

"Well, maybe he'll be something better next time," said Emery Ann.

"Do you believe in that?" I asked her.

"Forzino," said she.

Emery Ann was not talking Italian. It was the Yankee which, being interpreted, means "As far as I know."

And that is as far as a Yankee, or anybody else, can go.

As far as we know, why shouldn't it be?

Why these pains of life and death for things for which there is to be nothing " better next time"?

I wonder if anybody ever suggested, as a solution of the development question, the idea of *spiritual* " selection." We hear enough of " natural selection," and of how it may be that whole races live and propagate and die, struggling toward an attainment of more perfect organization, to be realized after they are dust or fossil.

What of the seed of life itself?

What good does it do the mollusk that there is to be a vertebrate by and by? or the monkey that there are men to come? Or men, in their turn, that there are to be sons of God again upon the earth when their mistakes and half-developments are over?

What if no life is ever lost? If God giveth it a body, — to every seed its own, — as it pleaseth him, over and over, up and on?

Two things stand right up in the way.

Deaths also; over and over.

Forgetfulness.

But then, — "forzino," again. *How* far do **we** know?

Only the dead can tell what death has been. It may have been — many times — an ecstasy.

Emery Ann's "forzino" set me out on this quest.

Pain only gets a soul when it comes to man; only begins to get something near it when it comes to the orders nearest human in their larger instincts. To other things it is always a surprise, not knowledge and reason: a surprise repeated from moment to moment, as long as it lasts. And a surprise is nothing except as you can turn round and look at it, or expect another.

A dog or a horse will cringe and howl, or quiver and snort with the terror which is the spiritual pain, when a danger that can *suggest*, approaches. A moth will burn itself half to cinder, and struggle back with its last strength into the flame again.

Suffering that is *all* of the body may not be, in our way of appreciation, suffering at all.

A man knows what is the matter with him. That is the trouble. He carries back the nerve-report to the centre of a grand and intense vitality. He has eaten of the tree of knowledge that is in the midst of the garden. The higher the civilization the greater the dread of injury and death. The Chinaman and the savage have little, or none at all.

Instantaneous pain is said to be no pain. There is neither expectation nor afterthought. A sudden, terrible hurt benumbs itself. It is too swift and strong. We do not know what has happened to us. It is after we begin to find out, and the mind takes part, — remembers, anticipates, imagines, compares, watches, — that the agony begins. It is a thing of the spirit.

It may be that we only, who can make of it a sacrament, are baptized into the full intimacy of suffering. It may be that for any creature who can approach our knowledge of it, it is by just so much, in them as in us, the working toward a "far more exceeding glory."

God is merciful. He takes care of his own mysteries. He gives to nothing more than it can bear, or more than shall be good.

Perhaps the chief wonder, after a great physical hurt, is that it had not been harder to endure.

There are blessed laws of alleviation; bounds beyond which are insensibility and rest; possibly, even, as heat and cold at their excessive points are one,— as great joy is a pang, and deep grief a strange blessedness, — there may be also an agony to rapture, known only to them who are taken into the mystery. There is always circumstance; the special providing for each experience, which is never forgotten; that which makes us say afterward, "If it had not been just so; if there had been a little more, or a little different!" It is never more; it is never different; it is always just what we can bear.

God is gracious, not to our souls only, but to our bodies; "not suffering any to be tempted" — tried, proven — "beyond that they are able;" but making always "some way of escape."

We can leave it all with Him.

If the "whole creation travaileth in pain together," it is surely "for the glory which shall be revealed."

But then, besides, the forgetfulness; the blank, behind and before!

If life has climbed so, why should we not remember the steps?

Perhaps we shall come to it, when *all* the glory is revealed. Perhaps the further we go, — the more we include, — the further we shall remember back.

Meantime, at this moment, we do know what nothing less than human can. We can divine the life that is below us; all its meanings are ours. The insect in the sunshine has, perhaps, in its own little atom of consciousness, no more positive sensation of its separate joy, than the man has, looking on; reading it so, and bringing it back for comparison to some sense of his own, included in his larger being. Somewhere in him is just this very pleasantness: where did he get it? The insect knows nothing of *his* gladness.

Somewhere in him — the man — is the flight and freedom of the bird in the air; the cool delight of the fish in the sea-depths; the bright, brisk busyness of the squirrel in the still, green wood. He knows it all.

Why does the child love better than anything the

stories of little lives like these; the pretty fables about dormice and lizards, ants and butterflies, bees and robins?

I don't pretend to declare why; I don't assert anything; I only say, as Emery Ann does, — "forzino!"

Above, they know us as we know these. We shall come, some time, to know even as we are known. Then we shall hold it — perhaps remember it — all.

I said something of this to Emery Ann. Not as I have said it here, but just in the way of common talk.

"You see," I suggested, as to the question of pain, "everything isn't always as bad as it seems. What we have never tried ourselves, we cannot tell about. Doctors say that a good deal that looks like terrible suffering — spasms, and such things — may be mere muscular action."

"That's very comfortin' — to the doctors," said Emery Ann. "They've tried 'em, perhaps. But it don't take a doctor to tell that things show for more'n they are. Why, bare ugliness does. Everybody gets along with their own; but I've noticed folks, — I don't mind *homeliness*, now, any more than I do kitchen chairs, if they are clean and whole, and set straight; but I can't bear faces that seem to want clearin' up, — well, with *mouths*, say, that you'd think they'd hate to keep their own tongues inside of. And as to noises and fuss, I've seen a piece of work made over takin' a nap, with jerkin' and snorin', that you'd say was fits if you'd never come across it before. I guess it's pretty near right, most of it; things are made frightful that we'd better try to keep clear of. At any rate, we can't fix it now, if it isn't."

Emery Ann is never uneasy about anything that she can't " fix ; " what she can, she has no peace of mind with till it is done. She doesn't fix her paragraphs though; she drops in her prepositions and her objective cases just when she happens to get hold of them, and her relative pronouns set up for themselves in sentences of their own, whether they ever had any antecedents or not.

Aunt Hetty Maria has been down to stay a fortnight with us. She and mother have been so comfortable together.

I don't think there is really anything nicer than old ladies; two together, especially.

The white caps, and the spectacles, and the slow, gentle ways that people get when they are old, and the Sabbath-peace that they sit down in, and the neighborliness of souls that have lived so many self-same years on the earth, and that may expect to begin young again so near together, — all this that is in mother's window, now, behind the larch boughs, is such a really beautiful thing!

I am afraid we are losing our old ladies out of New England, just as we are losing our peaches; the finest flavor of autumn time. Nobody seems to realize it. People are so taken up with looking for the *coming* woman, that they forget all about the *going* one.

For that matter, we are in danger of losing our young ladies too. At first they won't let themselves be, any more than at last they will let themselves go, as they were meant to. So that freshness and simpleness, — gentle and beautiful fading, — by and by there will neither of them be seen, if things go on; but in their stead one universal, melancholy fadge and wrinkle, from sixteen to sixty.

Women used, at thirty-five or so, to put on modest, delicate, submissive little caps; and then they could grow gray or bald under them without a separate agony for every hair; now, when the locks bleach, instead of being accepted and worn, in their beautiful whiteness, as the light of heaven touching upon one's head, they are Mrs. S. A. Allened; and when they thin,— ah, worse contingency! — they are deployed painfully and insufficiently over the needful space, and a satire of unaccounted-for abundance pinned on behind or atop.

People used to find out ways of mellowing and sobering in their dress, too, as the woods begin to do in September, and so have their own especial beauty as well as the green June hers. There *were* things once that were "too young" for middle age to bedizen itself with. And there were things also, just as pretty in their time, that young girls had to grow to.

I won't say anything about manners; they can't be peeled off, or mucilaged on; what the soul puts forth, will be; and if it doesn't put forth, — well, we lose our peaches and our golden leaves.

Here it is; women may choose, — this or that; they must choose, and take the consequences.

They may ripen their beautiful elder womanhood, fair with its quiet and content, noble and sweet with its larger life and loving, that gives us at last the real, dear old lady, and without which the dear old lady can never be; or they may hold on desperately as old girls, and wrinkle up just as they are; that way makes the Mrs. Skewtons. You can't have results without processes; you have got to make up your mind deliberately, when you come to the crest-line of life, in what fashion you will go down into the years.

There is a time, no doubt, when it seems sad and hard; when the path first turns, and the eastward heaven of youth lies behind the hill; when the glad little brooks begin to run the other way, instead of leaping to meet you; but go on, like one of God's women; it shall be an easy and tender slope under your feet; and the lowering sun shall shine upon your steadfast face to glorify it, and at the foot is the broad, sweet valley, and the river of your full, deep peace.

There is where my dear little mother has helped me so. It is beautiful going on just after her. And when I sit and look at the two there in her window, with their work and their caps and their cosiness, and hear them say to each other what a little while ago it seems, — the time before their lives began to run apart, — it is an outing that I can't get any other way; a reaching on, by something like heaven's own counting, over the years, to the time when nothing shall seem far back or away, or tedious to have been borne; and heaven itself shall be the nearest of all.

I read them my thinkings about Pain and Change, when I had written them down.

"Yes," said Aunt Hetty Maria. "If only *God* made all the pain, and gave it to us. But what about the pains we have *earned?* The pains of our sins?"

Mother spoke out, then; quick, before I could.

"Why, Hetty Maria, the thief got that answered

for us. And the Lord gave him part of his own peace, and promised him Paradise."

The cross of Love is close beside the cross of Sin. Jesus hung between the malefactors.

They "knew not what they did;" God knew, and meant it so.

VIII.

INTO DARK CLOSETS AND NEIGHBOR-HOUSES.

"Don't ever do that," said Aunt Hetty Maria. "Carry your candle as straight as you can, but never go prowling back into dark closets to look after mischief that you haven't done."

"It's clear fidget, I know," said mother; "but I've done it many a time myself."

I had been looking for something in the little clothes-room. I knew perfectly well that my candle hadn't snapped while I was there, and that I hadn't held it near anything; and yet, after I brought it back to mother's room, and gave her the roll of linen she wanted, I went quietly to the closet again, and shut myself in, in the dark, and looked. When I came back the second time and sat down, Aunt Hetty Maria said that.

"Don't do it," she repeated. "Clear fidget is the

worst thing you can give up to. It'll come back at times when you *can't* satisfy yourself. It's a way you get into, and it'll follow you up. Don't get out of bed to see if you have locked the door when you know there isn't one chance in a hundred that you haven't. Don't pull your letter open to see if the money is safe and right, when you know you had it in your hand to put in and it can't be anywhere else. Don't keep making crazy dives into your pocket and bags, to see if your purse and your keys are there, after you've started on your journey, and you can't help it if they aint. It's an awful habit, I tell you. You'll go back into actions and reasons and happenings, just so; into trouble, and sickness, and death too. Looking after what never was in 'em; and doubting what you know there certainly was. I tell you, for I know."

Aunt Hetty Maria had had troubles in her life, notwithstanding the silk gown and the white caps, and the looking-up-to of all Dearwood. There were things she wasn't sure she hadn't made mistakes in, though she was a woman who had always tried thoroughly to do her duty. Perhaps in some other place I shall say more of what I know about it. I understood enough about it then, to feel that she spoke out of a deep place, and that the strong sense that advised me against the "clear fidgets" had had sore battles to fight against them, before it stood up in her so, commanding them all down.

"If I had my life to live over again, there's no rule I'd lay down for myself firmer. And that's why I speak to you."

As if I had *my* life to live — at thirty-eight!

And, yet — as if I hadn't!

I think, sometimes, we don't any of us find out how to live till we have pretty well used up — spoiled, perhaps — one life.

Did anybody ever knit a perfect stocking, right off, at the first learning? Isn't the first experiment a tangle, more or less, of dropped stitches, run all through, or twisted in the picking up; of puckers and stretches, — unpremeditated and misplaced widenings out and narrowings in?

Aren't there patient eyes over the needles, perhaps, in our life-learnings? Is all the yarn spoiled in conquering the stitch? Are we to *wear* our first poor work, inevitably and always? Or when, out of the knowledge gained at it, we can accomplish a better, shall it not be given us to do and to possess, and the old puckers be quietly unravelled for us and laid away out of our sight?

If mother and Aunt Hetty Maria give me loving and watchful counsel at thirty-eight, looking upon all these years of mine as a mere "setting up," how will the good angels, out of their deep eternity and its holy wisdoms, look at theirs?

The very calm and beauty that sits upon them now, — is it not the smoothing out for a fair and glad beginning again?

"Don't go back into the dark closets!"

It was a dear, bright word to me. Perhaps it is the word that will be said to us in heaven, when we come out into the light there that is fulfilling and absolving love. Perhaps we shall be comforted and forgiven beyond what we can think or hope.

———

Rose Noble came in this morning.

I think it is one of the comforts of not being very rich people, that your friends talk *out* to you more, of any little plans or perplexities they may have, and with which money, as the world runs, must necessarily have so much to do.

Whether the old dress is worth making over; what sort of carpet would turn out the best and cheapest; or, if the dress is quite worn out, or the carpet can't be had,— the want and the way to bear it. They will speak of these things, which are the day's burden or interest, sure of your sympathy; sure, also, that they can, by no distant possibility, be seeming to dream of anything else. It is the comfort the poor and the moderately well-off have together; and which the rich, busy only with spending, or suspicious of wishfulness, are shut out from.

I know so much about Rose Noble and her mother; it is quite as if their lives were added on to mine. Lives that open into each other so are like houses with a door between. .

Isn't that an outing?

I think, all up and down the heavenly streets, they

build their dwellings so. I think, from God unto "the least of these," spirits stand open, one to another, and world to world. "I am the Door," says the Lord. "By me ye shall go in and out and find pasture." "That they also may be one in us, as I in thee, and thou in me."

I am glad to think we can begin it here.

I know all about them, — the Nobles; their plans and their makings out; what Rose has done, and what she has laid out for herself to do; and what the hope of her life is, after that.

The hope began when she was teaching school in western Ohio. She met Robert Haile there, a man working with an object in his life as well; a debt to pay back before he can begin to count for himself. When he can do that, he will not be afraid to take a wife and count for her also.

I said I knew all about Rose. That was true; as to Robert, I don't know all; not quite all that she does; and there is a something which Rose herself does not fully know yet, but for which she waits till he shall have it all to tell. He is thirty years old, and it is a story of his early youth. A dark closet, perhaps, where he *did* leave something smouldering. But she is not afraid. She knows him as he is.

Rose has kept school ever since she was sixteen years old; what she has determined to do before she ever marries or "counts up" in any way for herself, is to buy the little house for her mother that they live in now. She has got three hundred dollars more to save to do it. That doesn't seem much towards the price of a house, but it is a little one, and she has saved it all by fifties and hundreds, out of her school-keeping, from year to year. In the mean while they have to live; and things wear out; and Rose won't let them grow *too* shabby, to spoil so the pretty idea of the home she is working to keep for good and all.

So it was the sitting-room carpet that was worrying her now.

"They are so dear, you see. It will cost forty-five dollars. I don't talk to mother about it; I've come to you. If I do make up my mind to get it, it must seem easy, or she wouldn't take any comfort in it. Patience, I wonder if there's always a prophecy in names!

There certainly was in yours; and in Emery Ann's; how do you suppose mine happened?"

"Rose — Noble," I said, slowly; "why *shouldn't* it have happened?"

I thought of her fresh, sweet nature, and of the something deep and grand there is in it also, to which the freshness and sweetness are a mere outward adding. The *born* name, and the *given* name; they are precisely as they should be.

"It makes you think of the golden old times," said Rose. "Of the full pouches, and the princely givings. I wish there were a magic in my name. I wish whenever it were spoken a real rose-noble might drop down. Then I shouldn't have to count yards and shillings. Then, you see, — O Patience, it might be nearly here, the time we're waiting for!"

I saw that something more than common was on Rose's mind.

I didn't want to ask; and I didn't want to interrupt, if she chose to say more; so I sat silent.

"He might come this fall; *his* work is nearly done. I think he will come. But I can't possibly be ready with my part. I must leave mother and Katie comfortable, and you see I do want lots of little things myself, — besides the big ones. Patience, — if it's one ridiculous thing more than another, just this minute, — I'm such a goose, — it's — a band of back hair!"

I didn't think Rose was a goose.

I looked at her pretty head, with its bright hair, not very long, — she had had a fever from over-work a year and a half ago, and it had been cut short, — and so fine that its real thickness hardly told; so that although when she brushed it out it was light and full and shining, and looked ever so much, it would compress itself with the least little twist, like a skein of floss, and show for nothing.

I didn't blame her a bit, when other girls were wearing whole manufactures of hair-work that hardly let the original foundation betray itself at all, as to what it was or was not, for wishing just for a little more *like* hers, to make the story good, as it was really meant to be, and might be, by and by. And Dr. Haile coming before long, at least to see her.

And yet I do, on principle, hate false hair.

Only, it is a thing to wear now, as much as caps or bonnets; and everybody knows. Indeed, you *have* to wear it *instead* of bonnets, or else look so scooped out.

I don't know where the line is. A *great deal* is bad and frivolous and extravagant and worldly-minded; but a *little*,—just what Rose Noble wanted to make her head graceful and pretty, somewhat after the taste of the time, — well, I give it up, as I have to give up many puzzles; things that begin blamelessly enough, but end all wrong, and carry the world by the ears into all sorts of snarls.

Any way, I don't think Rose Noble was so very silly. And I told her so.

But then, she couldn't spend ten dollars for it. That ended the matter.

It was only a wish, given up to stronger and dearer claims. If that were the settling of such points, always! I suppose in that case, though, there would be precious little back hair worn, except what grew. And we should all look well enough.

I think, very likely, there are moral questions that can't be generalized. Special decisions must make up the broad result and answer. If everybody marks their own inch, the line will be drawn all round the world. Up and down, perhaps, like an isothermal; but it will be there, as true as conscience or science can make it.

That reminds me. I was thinking of that word, "conscience," the other day. Of the "con" of it. "Together." "With." Together with whom? What makes *con*science different from other knowing? What but God's knowledge joined to ours? The very contact of the human and Divine?

Rose Noble laughed, with a tear in her eye, at her own silliness; but it was very pathetic to me. So many "little things,—besides the big ones," were wanting in her young life, of which other careless lives were full.

I was quite sad about it after she had gone. I sat still half an hour, thinking it over and over. Some people had aunts and uncles, if not fathers and mothers, who could give them the little embellishments and opportunities of youth. Even I, more than half as old again, and past caring for much, of these outside things, had Eliphalet and Gertrude to be thoughtful for me when it wouldn't do for me to be thoughtful or wishful for myself; to give me a new pin at Christmas, and a silk dress on a birthday, or when they went shopping in New York; even to ask me — if I hadn't broken my bones and blundered out of it — to go to Europe with them.

I could think of so many people who wanted what they couldn't possibly get, and nobody would be likely to give them as long as they lived. Mrs. Shreve, who was "worrying through the summer" with an old cooking-stove that spoiled all her cake, and wouldn't heat her flat-irons; Mrs. Noble and Rose, wanting to carpet their sitting-room and put new curtains in the best bedroom; and obliged to choose between the two; people poorer than these, with real suffering wants, all around us; oh, what a wanting world it was!

I didn't know as outings into such a world, unless one could go with Haroun Al Raschid power, were worth having, after all.

All at once, I caught myself up.

"I never shall have a better chance!" I said, out

loud. "Unless — something should happen that would take the heart wholly out of everything. I truly believe I'm just about down-hearted enough."

And so I went and got the packet, which I had fairly forgotten since I had been able to be about the house.

It wasn't much to open; it was soon untied.

A little note from Eliphalet, and — two little common blue-covered books.

An account, opened at the Third National Bank of Boston, with a deposit of three thousand dollars to the credit of Patience Strong!

And a cheque-book, to draw the money out with.

IX.

INTO THE MIDDLES.

That was nice of Eliphalet. And so knowing. So much better than a certificate of stock, to draw a dividend on twice a year, and never feel the full three thousand dollars' worth of abundance unless I should happen to live some eight or ten years longer, be lucky in my shares, and keep a running account in my head, in a "House that Jack built" fashion, of the extra good it had done me. It was as much better as fifty coppers, all one's own, to spend, used to be than the rare silver half dollar given to "lay by." It was a clear piece of citron, to eat right up, instead of waiting for it in little bits, cooked and spoiled, in the cake. It is so delightful, once in a while, not to mind the proper way, or be wise and prudent, but to be as foolish and happy and unproper as one pleases. Eliphalet remembers old times, and knows that we don't outgrow, but only overgrow, many things. Especially we women.

"It would have cost me that, and more," — the trip to Europe for which I substituted my trip down the trammel staircase, — so he wrote in his note. "Therefore, do just what you like with it. Invest it, come out to Europe after us, or spend it all in gimp and sugar-plums."

Now, then, couldn't I have outings?

Could I, though? Just where I most wanted to go? Into wishes and wants, — into hopes and troubles? Into Mrs. Shreve's kitchen, with a new Perfect Rapture cooking-stove and a man to set it up? Into Mrs. Noble's parlor and bedroom, with carpet and curtains?

When I came to think of it, I'd got the lever, but I wasn't so sure of a place to plant it, — without hurting anybody.

Not right down on any quick, tender pride, or delicate self-respect and independence. That wouldn't do.

I must take care that my dollars didn't get in my way.

First, I made mother solemnly promise never to tell, — until I did.

Then I laid awake the best part of three nights, plotting and planning. Taking my share of the world's skein to unravel; the how to make ends meet. What everything and every soul is busy about, one way and another, from the least to the Highest; from the bringing together of the grub and the green leaf to the lifting of men's souls up into the Heart of God.

There is this and that; cotton on one side of the world, machines on the other, — coffee there, dry goods and iron and Yankee notions here; men, women and children there, starved and overcrowded, — work and wide lands out here, and yonder.

There are the homely " two ends, " income and out-go; there is money in pockets, want in bodies and souls; there is a word to say, and an ear straining to hear it; the world is running round and round. It is in great and small, grave and grotesque; the kitten after its own tail; the baby trying to get its big toe into its mouth; the mystic symbol of the serpent; the planet wheeling round the sun; the fiery beauty of the zodiac.

I think, what with planning and sleepiness, I was a little feverish and confused perhaps; all these things ran through my head in such curious associations.

My little bit was only this, — our side of the way and over across; I and my bank-book here; the Shreves and the Nobles, and their worries and puzzles there. How should I get the two together?

I felt myself dreadfully outside, all at once, with my three thousand dollars. How should I get in, — I who thought at first I had got tickets for everywhere?

Finally, and in the first place, I made up my mind that I must learn German. Rose Noble knew it, and I didn't.

Out under the beeches in the old garden, while the summer weather lasted; while Rose's school had long vacation, and she was busy making pretty nightgowns and under-robings. I could help her whip and hem, while I grated consonants between my tonsils, and learned long sentences in which the nouns were centipedes and the verbs were nobody knows where. And over the German and our needlework, we should grow intimate,—more intimate than ever,—and I should find some crafty and blessed way of "putting it,"—the rest of it, the little things and the big things, bit by bit,—that even pride could not resist; that, in truth, it could have nothing whatever, by any pretence, to do with. It would be like a game of "solitaire,"—"patience," as they call it in the English novels; laying this card carefully on that, looking through and through the position, catching my chances and my sequences, and making it all out gloriously at last, with my king and queen at top.

"I feel as if it was *my* story," I said to mother, who came into my room "visiting."

I wonder if anybody else has that way of mother's of talking about "visiting"?

She comes in between her busy times,—while the cake is baking, perhaps, or Emery Ann is sweeping her room, or in the odd minutes before dinner, or the twilight after tea,—and she sits down and says she has come to "visit a little" with me.

They had that way at Dearwood,—the sisters in

the old house; Aunt Hetty Maria has it too; but it doesn't sound so sweet from anybody as from mother. She comes so close, and so kindly; her visiting is right into your thoughts and your heart. It makes me think of the "gentle visitings" I remember in some old hymn. I think that if she were gone away out of the body, she would still come and visit me so.

"Well, it *is* your story," she said to me in reply. "You're living right into it. You're putting yourself into the middle of it. That's all that makes anything our story. The same story would be anybody's else if they could stand where we do to look at it. It's the pleasantness of books, and —"

"In the middle, — yes." I interrupted mother. The word struck me. "God is in the middle. Everybody's story is his."

"And it's the 'joy' we 'enter into,'" said mother, finishing her sentence, and weaving in her word and thought with mine. "Isn't it?"

"Loving the neighbor as one's self. The fulfilling of the whole law; the perfect rounding of the circle. Standing in the middle, beside God. Self is only the centre-point. We can put it where we please. There was 'an angel standing in the sun.'"

Mother reached over and took up the Bible that was on my little table.

"I wanted to see," she said, pleasantly, after she had found the place. "Why, it's a kind of a wonder, child! It comes like what we were saying." And then she read :—

"'He cried out with a loud voice, saying to all the fowls that fly in the midst of heaven, Come and gather yourselves together unto the supper of the great God.' It fits right in, Patience."

"It always does come so, mother. One part is never put into my head, that the other doesn't fit right on, and tell more. It fits to the old things too. It shows the pattern they were all cut out to. 'The fowls that fly in the midst of heaven.' The living knowledges and thoughts that go and come all through the heavens and between all souls. The bird-meaning. You remember, mother?"

"That was the supper they couldn't come to who were taken up with their own; their little bits of land,

and their wives, and their merchandise. But out of the highways and hedges they came. Those who had nothing. It's the rich that can 'hardly enter in.'"

"If they're in the 'middle' of nothing but their riches. Or their plans, or their pleasures, or their cleverness, or their prettiness. Yes, it's the middle that signifies. If you're in the wrong middle, move right out of it; find a new one; they're all around; everything is a middle."

I went on, thinking it out so, and brushing my hair. Mother had come visiting while I was getting ready for bed. They are dear little visiting times then; then, and at the early morning, when we are beginning new together, and the first thing is to find each other for a minute. It has been so ever since I was a little child. I believe it will be so when we begin new together by and by. The first thing will be to find each other,— to look in each other's morning faces. Everything is a sign, and God will make it all come true.

X.

INTO THE SUNSHINE.

It was so lovely this morning that we could not be content even under the old beeches. It was a sort of a truant day. Everything seemed to say, "Out! further!" One could rest in nothing, there was so much all about and beyond. The beauty was like a field of pasture fruit; it was impossible to stop to pick, it spread so wide to lure you on. The whole world was greedy with gladness. It was like the poorhouse boy, — only from very fulness, not denial, — sighing to itself and forth into the broad air that held it warm: "More! more!"

The little grasses and late clovers; the leaves, crisp and clean with dews and searching chemistries of light, and all alert with the spring that is in living things; the tall, lithe stems of the young trees, and the trunks of old ones mighty with their longer glad aspiring that was turned to solid strength; the glistening, restless clouds, the little winds of heaven like happy breaths,—everything panted and stirred and uplifted itself with an ecstasy that was at once replete and insatiate. The globe itself seemed to revel in blue space. It must needs roll on. One could almost feel how it would be impossible to lie so at a still point of bliss. The glad, golden orbit was accounted for.

Down the lane, the wild grape-vines had heaped up banks of living green over the low, old wall; the creepers tossed their grace and glory from tree to tree; the clematis was cloudy-white with blossom; the ferns were plumy and fragrant in every little angle; and the dear little life everlasting, with its delicate, mystical odor, was plenty under foot. The blackberries were full and sweet with their dark wine, and the scent of the pines and the cedars came up to meet you from the wood.

"We must go down there," said Rose.

"Shall we stop *anywhere?*" said I. "It's a day to go and seek a summer-fortune."

So I picked up "Ahn" and the "Lesebuch," and

we went down. Down into the cool and damp by the brown brook; over and up, into the spicy stillness of the evergreen pasture; close in, among the cedars, against the "shadow of the great rock."

The path brought up here; or we might have walked on until,—well, at least until some dusty turnpike stopped us. The rock was better. It was the best thing about this lane and wood-path that it had a natural pause and end. I like an upshot. Else you keep on,—with many other things as well as green lanes,—till the turnpike runs across, and the green wood shows its limits, and the beauty is all over.

I said a bit by heart, out of the "Lesebuch." "Abraham baüte einen altar." And I declined the dreadful little German article that stickles so for all its cases like any grown-up, significant word. And then Rose told me a little about substantive declensions.

I began to see the fog. I knew I had not got into it, so I held my peace. But I saw it was coming. That is the reason it is so much harder for grown people to learn a language, or any new thing. A child just takes the one step set for him, never counting on, or thinking how many more there may be, or what they have to do with each other. We grown-up simpletons anticipate, analyze, and try to get hold of the theory, and muddle our brains. Therefore, also, we must become "as little children," to learn the kingdom of heaven.

"I'm not discouraged *yet*, Rose; but I wish to tell you that I know it's there."

"What, discouragement?"

"Yes; the climax of it; there's always a climax of discouragement in everything. When you get into the thick of it, and can't see how, or if ever, you're coming out. It's in a poem, or a story, or a sermon, or a painting, or a piece of music, or a dress-fitting, or a house-cleaning, or a *living*. It's always there; and you've got to run against it, and have your tussle with it. Then, all at once, if you're blessed, you come out of it, into the clear daylight, and wonder where the dark was. It's the miracle worked in everything. It's the opening to the knocking. It's the 'borning,' as the little child said."

"That's a very true thing, Patience. I'm glad you've said it. Only — I can't help wondering, once in a while, if some people don't have to live all their lives in a climax."

"I never heard of but one person who did," said I, "and that was Mr. Micawber. And you know how it was disposed of, simply enough, for him. 'If he is going to be continually arrested, his friends have just got to be continually bailing him out,' says Aunt Betsy. Dickens put it in extreme, as his way is, but he puts the very doctrine of heaven into it, — which is also his way."

"Rose," I began again, after a minute or two, "I wish you and I had been children together; or else that you were child enough now to believe in a fairy story."

"Why?" asked Rose.

"Because then we should have got used to spending our coppers together, and dividing our nuts and candies, and shouldn't think anything of it; and because I've got a kind of a fairy story to tell. Somebody gave me a nut, and I've cracked it; and it's a good deal too much for one. And fairy gifts don't keep, you know. Rose, when you are married, I *don't* mean to give you a silver flat-iron or watering-pot, or — a parlor pitchfork and spoolrake—"

"What *are* you talking about?"

"Pitchforks? Spoolrakes? Why, the newest presents for brides, to be sure. Silver things to keep hung up by your work-table, and round everywhere, to reach after whatever tumbles down and rolls away just when you want it, and where you can't get it; or for what is out of arm's-length when you've got your lap full. If they haven't got 'em yet, they will by that time. They've invented everything else. I'm not going to give you any of these things; and you've got your grandmother's spoons. So I want, — *instead*, — it's a fairy story, you see, — to go a day's shopping with you, dear. Just *one* day. I want a real good outing, you see; and besides that, my pocket's burnt all through and through."

Where had all my beautiful craft gone to, and my game of patience?

I couldn't help it; it was just like me; my heart

and my pocket *were* burning; how could I wait till I could say it in German, and Rose in a climax all the while?

And besides that, I said before, it was a morning of outings. The whole world was reaching, and giving, and asking, and brimful, and running over.

But the open-hearted day was on all sides. She was touched and tuned with it, as well as I. She wasn't "Rose Noble," either, for nothing.

Her face was sweet, and bright, and surprised, with a thankful pleasure, as if some little sunshower had fallen; and there was a high, generous understanding in her eyes.

And she said, simply: —

"I can't refuse you the ' more blessed' -ness, Pashie, can I?"

It was all right, and very well; and the glad outgoing day had made me do it, and fixed it all, a great deal better than I could have planned. For there was plenty to do, somehow, by and by.

When we came home we found Mrs. Shreve sitting with mother. They had been laughing till there they both sat, wiping their spectacles. Mrs. Shreve was quivering yet.

"Why, what is it, little mother?"

And so they told it over again. How Mrs. Shreve's new, green Irish girl — "I shall always have a new girl and a raw one, as long as I have my old stove," she said, as chipper as ever for all that — had been found crying at the stairs. She didn't know how to go up and down. She'd never learned on anything but a ladder, at home, and had come straight from shipboard.

"It only shows," said mother, when we had got a little over it again, "the things we *do* learn, without realizing. We have to begin when we're babies, that's certain."

"And we never know what we're laying up for," said Mrs. Shreve. "I suppose it'll be so between this world and the next, in things we never think of."

"In just this very thing," said I, seized suddenly with the meaning. "There are stairs between the stories, — if we knew how to use them."

"Spirits crying at the bottom, — and spirits crying

at the top, perhaps, and only the angels knowing how to go up and down," said mother, gently.

"I think," said Rose, "the stairs we learn on are the stairs between the stories here, — between the different human lives."

"I knew I should get it out of you," said Mrs. Shreve. "That's what I came and told the story for. I didn't know *what* it was, but I had a feeling of something in it, besides the fun. And you always have the thing that's wanted, — cut and dried, and bottled and labelled. There's always herbs and cordial in this house, if everybody else is out."

XI.

INTO THE SHOPS.

Nobody would believe what an excitement it was to me, that day's going to Boston.

In the first place, I had not been away from home before, except to go to church, since I broke my leg. And then, almost anything, if you don't do it very often, and if most times your days are taken up with little busy, dutiful doings, makes a holiday, especially if you are hearty and thorough about it.

People who live ten miles or so from the city, and three-quarters of a mile out of the railway village, — who don't keep any horses and carriages, and don't spend money, usually, till they have thought at least twice about it, — get the full good of going to Boston. They begin over night. They make their memorandum, and their calculations; these last to be upset and twisted and reversed next day by shop experience and all the four parts of arithmetic, until, if it don't end in wholly losing one's head, and getting a general wild, reckless impression that one is simply absorbed with one's purse, as a very helpless and inconsiderable unit, voluntarily contributed, and no more to be extricated, into the rush and whirl of that day's Washington Street, and that nothing will matter to anybody but general results, — one may congratulate one's self on rare presence of mind and tenacious individuality. There is the silk, so much a yard, cost of importation, — so many patterns in a piece, or a losing remnant, — so much at retail to pay a reasonable profit to honorable trade, — one price at all the stores, — what are you going to do? All political economy and commercial combination are against your simple-minded, little back-parlor plans and reckonings of last night.

But I was beginning with the pleasantness; I didn't mean to get into the craze. Sometimes you don't; sometimes everything falls right in. It is all match-grooved; you make all your connections; another time everything is unhitched.

We had a smooth day, — Rose and I; from the

ride down the shady Old Road, in Farmer Graitt's covered wagon, with our best bonnets on — (people who go every day or two keep "Boston bonnets" of a meaner sort; but if we didn't wear our best to Boston, when should we wear it?) — to the coming out at night, galvanized up to the arm-sizes with watchful consciousness in every little nerve and muscle of paper parcels various in shape and bulk, never to be lost feeling of till they were got safely home, and with only our elbows left to hold against our pocket-plackets for fear of the picks.

The waysides were blue with the midsummer flowers of the wild succory. The tanzy was getting golden tops. There was a little savor of sea-saltness in the air, that just tingled the nostrils delicately, and made a cordial of the light August wind. We met little boys with bare feet and big baskets, going up to the pastures, berrying. Round the railroad station were gentlemen in summer trowsers and waistcoats and straw hats, unfolding their morning papers; and ladies alighting from carriages, giving each other fresh morning greeting with fresh, bright faces

What a pretty world it was, — this side of it! How easily the day began, and might run on, and other days come after, just like this!

It was queer, though, to think of dear, good Mrs. Shreve, at home with her raw girl, and her pestering stove, and her ironing, on this gay, free day. And of people sick on beds, and people tired with night-watching, and people hard at work in dusty little shops, and mothers with arms full and houses waiting to be put to morning rights, and all the worry and ache and weariness that were surely about, somewhere. Only, people are so quiet about it! The world has learned to put up with so much! There are the houses, in which such manifold cares of life are going on, hushed, hanging no flag out, making no sign; nobody rushing out at the doors to proclaim a grievance, or protest against the careless comfort riding by.

Yet the whole world lies open, skyward; and no walls shut out the heavenly sight and ministering. No place, even, is mean to the angels; they come and bring their own glory with them.

This went through my mind, standing in the village waiting for the cars. There was little stir except what car-time made; and presently there would be a rush and a shriek and a bustle, and then in a minute, the still little place would be left to its own stillness as if it had just died. And it gives up the ghost so, every day.

It was something to be part of the ghost to-day. To be one of these for whom the fuss was made, and whom the little boys looked after, leaning over the bridge-rail; little boys, some of them, who never went to Boston in their lives; who stood at this end always, seeing the people go and return, and knowing that the great city lay at the further end of those two iron lines that curved off into the little wood beside the river.

Why, you can't move but you get so much to think of. You *are* in a middle continually, whether you will or no. It is spiritually and geometrically true.

The little birds sat on the telegraph wires. I wonder if they feel the thrill of the great words that run under them along their perch; and if they fly off suddenly to the woods to tell there what wonderful things are outside; or if they think the iron strings are spun through the air on purpose for them to roost on; and if so, what their great-great-grandmothers did without them?

Perhaps we rest on spiritual lines as wonderful; how do we know what quivers back and forth close by us, — what unseen force is in each thread we cling to?

There is a good deal in the spirit of things. It was so in the beautiful out-doors, the other day, when all things were giving and taking; it was so in the shops this morning, when everybody was having and spending. It didn't seem so much for me to have the silk measured off for Rose, — that we both decided would be so especially pretty for her, — as it would have done if I had gone alone and bought it, and brought it home with the formal parade of a present.

I let her pay in the street cars for both, with her ready small change; and it was several times, for I could not tax my weaker limb with too much walking about. And I let her settle for the dinner checks at Vinton's, while I finished my ice-cream. I never thanked her, or took any notice; it was all for granted that we were out on a holiday together, spending our coppers.

So she didn't mind, — so much, I mean, — when I paid at Hovey's. And then I didn't give her time to think of anything, except whether I was going to break my neck, or at least my leg again, as I plunged across Summer Street amongst the teams and carriages, threading myself in and out against the back wheels, and ran up into the carpet store.

"You see it's your mother's turn now, Rose, so hush up. I think, myself, it's the mothers that *ought* to have the wedding presents."

That was an inspiration. Rose couldn't refuse for her mother, and her mother couldn't refuse after Rose had accepted. I never thought of it till that minute, but it was one of the things that fayed right in, that blessed day.

"I don't know," said Rose, with a kind of a gasp in her breath as she whispered, — for the carpet gentleman had met us now, at the head of the stairs, — "but I feel as if I were going over Niagara Falls."

"Precisely; so what have you to do with it? It's the river's lookout. Can you show us some small-figured, ingrain carpets, — bright colors, — brown, with a little crimson, sir?"

I said it very glib, understanding myself perfectly, which I don't always do — at the right minute — when I go shopping. That's another difference in the days, and the state of brain; the memorandums may be all the same. I established the rapport directly, — between me and the salesman and the particular roll of carpet that was there, among those walls of rolls, like the statue in the marble. It is dreadful when a sort of fog comes over you just when you mean to make your wishes plain, — a distrust of the instant appreciation of your attendant, who, of course, in that case, instantly does *not* appreciate. It is your faith that fails; and so you stand before the mountain, — the whole enormous stock in trade, — and nothing moves; except, indeed, exactly the wrong things, which, if he's very obliging, he goes on with till you are ready to cry because you can't possibly stop him.

Now, it was rolled right down, — the very thing we had thought of and talked about; little bright, brown leaves, and red berries, twisted together over a mottled ground of quieter shades; well covered in the pattern, and well knit in the weaving; good to sweep and to wear, and lovely to look at.

"We'll send the express for it to-morrow morning," said I; and I left Rose sitting on a carpet-roll while I got away to the desk, to give the address and pay the bill.

That hadn't seemed much either; we were suited so quick, and there was so little chance for comparing and counting up.

Afterward, we were in and out at Mudge's, and Churchill & Watson's, and Holbrook's, — jolly and reckless as two little drops in the rapids, that had just as lief go anywhere now, among the rest, as how could we help it once we had got in? And we made up indiscriminate bundles together, she choosing, and I choosing, and both paying, till I knew she would never unravel the account of it, or know exactly how she happened to get half of them, — the big things and little. I didn't *say* anything about the two lace collars, or the half-dozen little vine-embroidered handkerchiefs, or the Balbriggan stockings, which she didn't know were eighteen dollars the dozen, but which I knew would be worth the money, and outlast all the rest she was buying. What business had she to interfere with my part of the parcels?

I never felt so bright, and so wicked, and so wise, and heart-happy, in all my life.

I couldn't smuggle in the "back hair" among the dry goods, so I took her deliberately away to West Street, among the waterfalls, and, — I can't think of any other word, — I "boosted" up her conscience to buy.

"If it wasn't more than six dollars, — just a little one, — *perhaps* she would."

And so we went in.

I had been there last winter with Aunt Hetty Maria, to get a frizette, so I felt as if I knew the plan. When you don't buy a thing more than once in a dozen years, it seems as if it stood out among the seller's transactions as it does among your own. At any rate, I knew them all well enough to-day. I felt intimate and privileged everywhere; for I had, — or had had, — a hundred and fifty dollars in my pocket, and twenty-eight hundred and fifty more at home, in the blue book.

XII.

INTO THE YEARS.

Rose was as shamefaced over the box of bands as if the man were used to blushes.

Of course there was nothing for six dollars,— scarcely for ten or twelve; though at last, finding that the law of increase in price was more according to the inch or two difference in lengths, than to the thickness, I matched the bright chestnut tint of the head that bent itself so mutely above the counter of falsities, with a soft, full fall of hair, not quite so fine or quite so long as those we had been looking at, but bright as Rose's own, and which the dealer said he would let us have for eleven dollars. "And cheap, too, for the shade everybody's wearing."

Rose lifted her head, and moved the box slightly from her. "You see it is no use," she said, "and perhaps it is just as well."

But I was so determined that day upon my wickedness.

I put the hair into her hand.

"See," said I, "the color is perfect,—better than those long ones. And I think we can come to some agreement. We are country ladies," I observed persuasively and confidentially to the hair-merchant, "and expect to make bargains, you know."

Meanwhile I had got out a five-dollar bill. I could have picked Rose's pocket, let alone my own, for all she would have noticed about it. Her head was down again. She didn't know what to do with the band of hair, or how to get rid of it. I believe she was getting vexed with me.

I held up the five-dollar note over her shoulder, between my thumbs and fingers. I nodded to the man.

"Call it six dollars," said I, as bold as Jack the Giant-Killer. "That was the price she had made up her mind to."

The man's eyes looked funny for a minute, between growing big suddenly and then twinkling. I don't think he ever had such extraordinary customers before.

"Well,—it *is* an odd length,—and wove in the old style, flat,—if it suits you, I'll *call* it six; though it's low, very low; and I shouldn't like the price to be told of."

No danger of Rose displaying her bargain, which she was so ashamed to make.

I took the thing from her, and gave it to the shopman to be put up; and with it, I tucked the five dollars into his hand.

She got out her little porte-monnaie, and paid the six; and that's all she knows about it to this day.

I have about come to the conclusion that—once in a great while—even a good, well-meaning action is all the more enjoyable if you have to put a little spice of iniquity into it.

Rose was very still, riding up that evening, in Farmer Graitt's wagon. Things seemed to be coming over her all at once with a sort of realizing sense. We had got out of the city whirl into the calm country again.

When she got down at her own gate and bade me good-night she said:—

"I don't half know what has possessed me to-day, Patience. What will mother say to it all?"

It was the naughty child coming home after the fun was over.

"Never you mind, Rosy," said I, as hardened as ever. "Don't tell her everything all at once. I'll come across to-morrow morning, and bear all the blame. And help make the carpet."

The next day was my birthday. I have got into a way of having birthdays lately. They always used to come, once in a while, but nowadays the whiles are shorter.

There was more than a plenty of time between them once; I got quite tired of being eight years old, I remember, before the day came when I could say I was nine; and I was thoroughly used to calling myself fifteen before the dignity of sixteen was laid upon me.

I was in no danger, then, of forgetting my age There was a real mile between each two milestones.

I travelled in a coach and four in those days; I could see the wheels go round, and count the little flowers by the wayside. At some point or other, unperceived of me, they took off the horses, and put on steam; and now, whiz! the milestones flash by me, till life seems sometimes nothing but a post and rail fence.

There is, really, such a thing as an " uncertain " age. It is a solemn fact that the time comes when you have to stop and calculate before you can tell the truth. Why, it is quite hard enough to remember the year of our Lord, — at least between January and July. No wonder they make a festival of the world's birthday. They have to. It is a mere practical necessity. Without it, the very planet would lose count and go adrift, like any other spinster. I hardly got used to 1867 before 1868 came; indeed, it seems queer still that we are in the sixties at all. I *realize* nothing farther down than the forties. The rest seems tacked on in a hurry. The years are as if they had been gathered before they were ripe; or like what I was talking about the other day, — the machine stitches that you don't have the comfort of *as* stitches; the first thing you know, you've got a seam.

That brings me back to this very, blessed birthday

of mine,— my thirty-ninth. There was another seam done,— I had only got to join off,— and I meant to have a holiday. I gave myself my own treat. I tyrannized over my little mother, and made her give up everything she had thought of,— the special raspberry-roll for dinner and the iced-cake for tea,— the making of them at least, that she was going to help Emery Ann with,— and come over with me, picnicing and carpet-sewing at the Nobles'. Emery Ann could make the raspberry-roll alone, and bring it after us at twelve o'clock.

We have a fashion round in our little neighborhood, — the Shreves, and the Nobles, and we,— of picnic visits. We did it before great surprise parties were invented. We would take our pie and our knitting-work, and " run in." It is a nice way. Especially if you choose a day when you know that the girl is gone, or any little domestic enterprise out of the cooking line, and adverse to it, is afoot; your knitting-work is nothing to lay by, you know; and you are running breadths, or setting up china before anybody notices; and the pie or the roasted ducks come in so ".pleasant and unexpected" at the end. For it is an understood point that though you bring a basket as big as a baby's wagon, and only produce four needles and a ball of yarn to account for it, and though everybody has to walk round it and over it twenty times, it shall be an utterly invisible and spiritual presence till the surprise comes out of it.

I killed two birds to-day; or I made two knots in the end of my seam.

I had something all ready in my pocket for Dickie Shreve; that is, for his mother, only she wouldn't know it. It was really a cooking-stove; but in fairy dealings, — which are all that can come of a fairy gift, — you never know exactly what you have or handle.

What I appeared to take out of my pocket and give to Dickie Shreve that morning — it happened nicely "by the way" as I meant it should, for we met him as we went across — was a year's railway ticket.

He was going to enter the School of Technology in September; and I expected to make a little expressman of him in his trips to and from the city. I told him so; that I should have books from Loring's, and things from dry-goods stores, and Brigham's rolls, and letters to post, and cheques to cash, and bills to pay, and worsteds to match, all winter long; so he needn't be obliged; he didn't know yet what he was coming to. I had made up my mind to have a claim upon him, and he would be tired enough of his bargain before he got through.

Season tickets *are* pretty dear on our branch, and I knew it would make the difference of the cooking-stove, and more, in Mrs. Shreve's plans. I saw a new suit of clothes in the perspective of Dick's eyes, as I snubbed him up in his thanks and sent him off.

The carpet arrived at Mrs. Noble's just as we did; and she didn't know which to let in first. Gammel was in a hurry, and the great roll was right in the doorway, and so were we. There were so many counter-excitements, and it was so exactly as bad for us as for her, blundering right upon this particular moment, that everything was got over without being really done at all; giving and taking, and blaming and thanking, and walking in and making welcome. Mrs. Noble never got farther, or clearer, than:—

"Well, I never did! Rose said — but I couldn't

have believed — what could possess you? I don't know a thing to say, — I haven't got a single word. Come right in, and lay off your things. I'm right down glad to see you, at any rate."

We hadn't anything to lay off but parasols, and then we all fell to cutting the cords and pulling away the heavy paper, and letting out the bright lengths over the floor.

"Well, who *would?*" began Mrs. Noble again. "I do declare, it's perfectly elegant! And I can't say a single word!" She was as sure of this as any speech-maker, and went on accordingly. "Why, you could most pick up those leaves, especially the light-shaded ones, — those maple-yellows. They look so raised. And it's such a good mixed ground; and the pattern all wove in so close and firm. Why, there won't be a pocket in it when it wears; and it never will wear. It'll turn over, and end for end, and any way. Well, there, — I haven't got a word!"

Sure enough, now she hadn't. She had said it till it had come true.

We had a beautiful time, cutting, and matching, and

sewing; only there wasn't half enough to do. There were only five long seams for four of us; and the ends to catch-stitch down, and the short pieces to put on for the side windows by the chimney. By the time Emery Ann and the raspberry roll came, we had got all through, and had spread it out and were walking on it.

"You might rake 'em up, all into one corner, they're so natural," Mrs. Noble began over again. "*I* shouldn't ever have lit on it. They'd have sold me some old thing in squares, or eggs, or diamonds. I'm so old-fashioned looking, you see; they keep things laid by for old women and out West. And you can't show 'em half you know, — that is, if you're at all polite. Paper hangings and carpets are the biggest trials to buy; I'd as lief be fed with a spoon."

It was such a real, good time. It was one of the best birthdays I had almost ever had, — this last of the thirties.

It was one of the life-outings; one that might have been hard and regretful, but filled brimful of sunshiny pleasantness for me to remember it always by.

I shan't be a bit afraid to go clear out — into forty.

XIII.

INTO THE NEW TESTAMENT PART OF IT.

Mother's birthday is just a fortnight after mine. For a little while, so, I feel, — after a fashion, — the oldest. At any rate, I am always her oldest child, and she is my youngest mother; for the mother is as many in her family, — separately and specially to each, — as God is in his world.

We are both in one month; the beautiful September My day is the very first, and hers is the fifteenth. I have the earliest touch of the autumn time upon me, and she is in the middle beauty.

For just these two weeks, we can pretend to count a whole year less of difference.

She tells me of those happy two weeks, of which the reminder is like a long birthday joy, reaching from mine to hers, and making it holy and beautiful all between; when she was not quite eighteen and I had come to belong to all the rest of her life, for always and always. I enter so into what it must have been for her, that it is as if I, too, had known motherhood. All mutual relations are like reflected rainbows. The first is straight from the sun; but the second is over against it and like unto it; and the one light is in them all.

We almost always make some plan that links our birthdays together and keeps them as one. We take the fortnight to do something pretty and extra for the house, beginning on my day, and finishing and setting up on hers; or we go to Dearwood, or to Boston, — to Eliphalet's, taking the pleasantness of the plan and the starting and anticipation for me, and the better pleasantness of the home-coming for her; and lay up thirteen days of things to talk over all winter, between. Or we have somebody to stay with us, and keep simple festival; without *their* knowing why, perhaps.

This time our hearts were in the same thing, — Rose Noble's little wedding havings; we had got into the middle of those. I had almost made the child believe that she might go on with what she knew she could do herself, and leave the rest to Providence, that had begun to bring things to bear, and was setting a hope for the bright October in both their hearts that would never be let to come quite to nought.

As for the school, Katie was to keep it up now, whenever she left it; so that made no difference.

And there was something I had got it into my head to do, that I could do best by way of helping Rose.

What would become of me if I had, — what does become of people, I wonder, who have, — thirty, or three hundred thousand to do with and to account for? My outings crowd so with these three thousand opportunities of mine. For I mean to spend them every one somehow; and put out *what they get* at interest. I shall have it all my life to be glad of; and the gladness of it shall be growing in other lives. Bank interest isn't the only interest, even in common, selfish money-using. A man failed and they took all his money away; that was all they could find though; he said he'd had forty years of good living, and they couldn't touch that.

How can I tell that I should be here to use it as it

came, — the little income, — two or three hundred a year? Or that some trouble of ours should not claim it, or sweep it all away? Or that I should keep my good mind even, and do with it the best it could do, and not be tempted too much, here and there, in my own living and having?

Of course I could fix it somehow, to all probability; I could endow, or bequeath; but I believe so in that other, living, interest, better than the dollars that grow out of dollars, and can only do dollars' worth as they come, after all. Nothing stops; percentage is only the sign of a realer thing. The box of ointment might have been turned into three hundred pence, and doled out here and there; but it was all poured on Jesus' head; and the perfume of it has come down into the whole world, and the years of our Lord, and has filled this room of the Father full.

I have got Seelie Rubb on my hands now. Of course. Why are we shown first one thing, and then another? First blue books full of money-orders; and then Seelie Rubbs, — if we're not to put this and that together?

Why shouldn't I spell after the Lord as fast as he puts his finger on the letters? Dollars — or any gifts — are only illuminated initials; the shine of them is only the leading to what comes next; all the little plain black print that joins the meaning on.

Seelie Rubb's little pale face and tired figure didn't stop under the locusts, and look over into our side-yard that very next Monday when I was shaking my duster out of the parlor window, without coming into my parsing and spelling. Everybody must study their own primer.

"Won't you come in?" said I. "You've had a long walk from the village."

She looked surprised. She had never been into our house in her life. She had come by twenty houses that morning that she had never been into.

The door stood open, and I went round and stepped out on the porch. She turned in at the gate, to answer me civilly within earshot.

"I don't know, — I guess not, — I'm very much obliged; I was out for a little fresh air. It's so different in the village, you see."

"Come right in, and have a glass of milk, Seelie. That's different in the village too."

I brought her some morning's milk, — we always set away one or two tumblers to cream over for drinking; you get the sweet top-flavor all through, so, — and a slice of mother's sponge cake on a plate.

"Why, you're very kind," said Seelie, simply. "I don't know as I ought to let you take the trouble. How pleasant it is here!"

She sat by the west window, up which the creepers came, and beyond which was the chestnut shade. It was different from Miss Widger's little shop, where she sat and worked at dress-making, and where a geranium pot and a great white cat with pink bows in its ears filled up the window-seat, and the dust of the street came drifting in.

"If shops didn't only have to be in villages!" Seelie said.

"Yes, if work could all be done in the pleasant green places! I think of that, sometimes, in the village and in town. How the work of the world overlays the world, and blots the color of it out. How men come with their mills and their blacksmithing into the woods by the rivers, and how other things have to come after, till everything is gravelled and planked and bricked and crowded up, and the beauty is buried, and a stone put over it. And yet the sweet earth with the seeds in it is underneath all the while, and the blue and the clouds are overhead, and it's always a place that *might be*, and that there are some scraps left of, — trees and water — and grass blades coming up between the bricks, — after all."

"If it was only the planks and the dust," said Seelie. "But it's getting pretty bad lately with Badsham's smoke, since he set the new chimneys going. They come right up out of the hollow, and so just send that yellow choke into our windows. Once or twice every day, — when they fire up or something, — its dreadful. It's bad for mother, too, since she had the pleurisy. Oh, it's another world the minute you get this side of the hill!"

I know how that is. I know how the woods and pastures meet you with their sweet breath, as you come down just ever so little over the crown.

"You're not busy now, then? The fall work hasn't come in much?"

"No. Miss Widger won't want me till about the twentieth. I wish she did. Then the fall hurry begins. I've been out, now, since the second week in August. I meant to have gone down East to my uncle's, for a vacation, but mother hasn't been well. I wish I could get her up here. It would do her a sight of good to come up and breathe a little. But she couldn't ever walk so far."

Green pastures and still waters! What that promise must be to so many!

I sent some sponge cake and some pears to Seelie's mother, and the rest of that day I thought it over, — till it fayed in.

"That's off my mind!" said mother, putting away the week's mending, and turning the stocking-basket bottom up.

"I don't know as there's any particular good in that," said Emery Ann. "Something else'll be onto it again directly. I've spent all my life in getting things off my mind."

"Well, that's it," said I. "That's living."

"Seems so," said Emery Ann, and went out of the room.

"Mother, I want to do something rather queer," I began, as soon as she had gone. "I've been thinking of it these two days. It's on *my* mind."

"Well, childie?" said mother, with faith and patience in her voice.

I didn't want to try them too far. She mightn't altogether like it, and quite reasonably.

"Would you mind? Would you think it very queer? I've looked at it till I can't tell. It's as straight as can be in a New Testament light."

"I hope my spectacles won't make it crooked then," said mother. As if *she* ever crooked anything!

"It's the Rubbs; Seelie and her mother. You know Seelie, in Miss Widger's little shop? The very thing that makes it queer is the New Testament part of it."

Mother smoothed her gown over her lap, and said

nothing; waiting quietly for me to end my shying about, and come to the New Testament part of it.

She smoothed her gown down so, when she was ready and attentive; when she had put her own affairs out of her thought for the minute, and waited to take in somebody's else; just as she might lay her work out of her hands, and smooth her lap to take a child up, and hear what it had got to say. I could talk out freer when it came to this pleasant sign of hers.

"I want to ask them right up here, mother, for a while. They're strangers, but I'd like to take them in. That's the queerness, — and the other part."

Then I went on, braver.

"You see they're choked out with Badsham's smoke. And Seelie got tired with her hot-weather work, and never got rested; her mother's been sick. And she crawls up here for a breath of pasture air, — and can't take it home to her mother in a basket. And it fits all round, as the right piece always does. Rose has got her dress-making to do, and we meant to help her along at any rate; and Seelie can measure and baste her here at home, and save her ever so much hindrance; and we can all be together, — all the birthday-time, motherdie, — in such a satisfaction!"

"Well, dearie, I see the New Testament part of it; but where's the queerness?"

And the darling little woman smoothed out her lap again, motherly and welcoming, and her face opened itself like the daylight, and — I couldn't see the queerness myself, now. It had all come into place, a part of the things that are; the *settled* things, that in a minute are no longer strange, but get an old look directly, as if they had been from the beginning.

I've got to skip over this fortnight, pretty much; I wish I hadn't. There was ever so much in it. Rose's pretty work, which Seelie said was a rest itself, after the fineries of mill-girls and servants; and the walks down the lane, and in the garden; and Mrs. Rubb's talks about down East, and their happy days, and their troubles, and their moving, and how they had been "put to it" to get on here; and Emery Ann's nice breakfasts, and dinners, and teas; and Mrs. Rubb's noticing of our old-fashioned backgammon table in the corner. — so odd and so handsome, —

that swivelled round and opened over, and had the little side cribs for the men and boxes, and was so pretty with the inlaying of two-colored woods; and mother finding out that she knew how, and was so fond of it, and used to play so much, only their board got broken first, and then lost in the moving; and their games together in blind man's holidays; and everything seeming so natural, as if they might have been friends or cousins, instead of strange people out of the village; and Mrs. Rubb's saying that there was "one more beautiful place in the world, and she shouldn't ever lose it nor forget it;" and their going home in Farmer Graitt's wagon, with some of Emery Ann's bread, and mother's cake, and a pair of roasted chickens, because their fire had been out for ten days; and a big basket of pears, and Porter apples, and tomatoes, and some Hubbard squashes under the seat, because we had more than we knew what to do with; and best of all with a color in Seelie's cheeks, and a look in both their faces, as if it was glad and worth while again to be alive.

This was the between-time; but I had something

kept back still, for the real birthday, when mother was her dear, bright fifty-seven.

I took her to walk in the warm sunset, — we were having beautiful days, and great, ripe harvest moons, — and we went away through the cedar woods till we came out on the Edge Rock, where our land ended, and a piece came in cornerwise, up out of the hollow, — a beautiful little piece, three acres and a half or so, of oak and maple woodland, — opening out on the other side upon the little twist of cross-road, and squaring so with our own boundaries further up.

Mother never cares to own things, — just *for* owning; but some time or other the old home-place would be Eliphalet's; and men like things square and shipshape; she knew he'd think of it by and by, and she'd often been half a mind to speak about it; but she'd rather buy it herself, if it should ever come convenient; and I knew she would like to *call* it hers a little while, too, for she always loved this rock, and the beautiful, billowy outlook over the trees, and she had memories with it.

Now, this land was Rose Noble's; a part of what

her father left her, separate from the old farm which was sold out in the early days of their trouble, and nobody had wanted it enough to give a good value for it, or it would probably have gone after the rest long ago; so they had sold some wood, and paid the taxes, and Rose laughed about her "real estate."

The other day, I bought it of her in mother's name, giving her four hundred and twenty-five dollars. And to-night I had the deed in my pocket; and while we stood there on the Edge Rock, and the maples were splendid in the sunshafts that shot through their bosoms and showed the first gleams of their ripening glory, — while everything was at its prettiest, and mother was saying, as she always did when she stood here, that there wasn't another spot on the whole farm like it, — I put the paper in her hand, and told her that the Little Red Wood-lot was her birthday gift.

XIV.

INTO GOD'S TREASURE-BOX.

I'm sure I didn't begin to know what I was undertaking when I set out to write down about the Outings.

Why, there is no end to them! They are the forever-beginnings. The very flow of the river of water of life, that cometh out of the Throne. To say all about them would be to make a Bible, or a world. Even all of them that there is in the very quietest life; for each touches and takes fast hold of the whole. Besides the think-outings, and the do-outings, and the give-outings, — which are life and love, and some simple shape of which we every one must discover in ourselves, — there are the come-outings, and the find-outings, and the grow-outings, and the turn-outings, — which are the wonderful gift and dealing and disclosure and providence of God, in and for and about us. It was for Life the Lord bade us "Watch!" Not for death and doom. It is to Life we are blind and unconscious; not knowing what hour He doth come.

It was a little thing, — to tell of after words like these, — that made me think of this so, just now.

It was a finding-out of myself. I have painted a little picture.

I didn't know as I could. I learned something about it years ago, at school, as all the girls did; just as I learned a little music, and left off practising gradually, after cares came and kept me busy, and the old piano gave out, and everybody's else had an octave and a half more, and the new, beautiful music was all written for the grand instruments. Besides which, after Aunt Judith came she couldn't bear the noise.

I think I always noticed lines and shades, and had an eye for what was true and in symmetry. And somehow it must have been "mulling" quietly in me, as a lesson does, learned over night and slept upon; gathering to itself little hints here and there, unconsciously; training and unfolding a possibility that sometime should come to the light suddenly. I suppose I never darned a stocking, or shaped the curves of a dress, or looped up a window-curtain, or, more than all, set delicate flower-stems in branching harmony, and made their bright tints lie against each other in the accord of color, so as to spell the meaning meant, without this art-instinct which is the translation of heavenly language, catching insensibly and laying up some new and beautiful phrase.

I suppose that eye and touch and feeling are all educated, by the commonest, teasing little every-day things; the trying to fit things and lay them straight; the making of beds; the setting of tables.

I suppose an orderly room, when we *make* the order, and have to study how, teaches a lesson in grouping and perspective, and Heaven only knows what more. That one cannot trim a bonnet without learning truths of lines and contrasts; that doing any one thing well — even setting stitches and plaiting frills — puts a key into one's hand to the opening of some other quite different secret; and that we can never know what may be to come out of the meanest drudgery.

The Lord hides away the seeds of wonderful, joyful life in us; and we sleep and wake, night and day; and they spring up and grow, we know not how.

At any rate, something put it into my head all at once that I should like to try to *make* the beautiful lines and touches that I studied every day in a certain little copy of Ellenreider's lovely cherub-picture of the "Gloria in Excelsis." Gertrude lent it to me when she went away, to hang in my room; and I have looked at it, and into it, ever since, until it has seemed to grow into my mind and apprehension, and become a real possession; as if I could put my finger right upon it anywhere, — on any secret of its beauty.

So now that I was rich, and could afford to try experiments, I went one day and bought paints and brushes, and a little square of canvas which I brought home and set up on a shelf, and looked at, wondering if there would ever be anything on it; if the little face and wings would really grow there upon the blank priming; and the beautiful meaning shine out at me.

And, without my knowing how, or whether I could

ever do it again, it has; and I have got the "Gloria in Excelsis" for my *very* own.

I have a feeling that I could do other things in the same way; that everything is linked together; that music and sculpture would come; and that it is not so bad a matter, after all, that we seem to get a glimpse of the many things, and scarcely to achieve the one, in these short lives of ours; since that in the little we are so surely laying hold of the much; and that, in our few and tiny steps upon the earth, we do draw the great globe itself toward us, with all its wealths, in every footfall.

We know not, verily, that which is laid up for us. There are such beautiful things *put by*. In God's house, and in God's time, there are such treasures. It comes true so, what I wished once when I was a little girl, and mother gave me some things out of an old trunk I watched her looking over. "If I could only have great boxes full of things saved up to pick out from always!"

The kingdom of heaven is like unto a householder. It has made me very glad, — with a new and large forth-looking and expectance,—just the painting of this little picture.

I have got a little easel now, in my window, and mother sits by, knitting, while I paint. I am doing autumn leaves, to burn upon the walls inside when the outside blaze is over. I have got the gold-brown of the hickory, and the deep bronze of the ash, and the amber and flame of the maple, and the shining crimson of the oak; and I am grouping them together, and unravelling their marvellous interweavings of glorious color, and matching and mocking them with umber and carmine, and sienna and vermilion; and finding one speech in the dead minerals and in the living leaves.

Mother is so pleased.

But her pleasure gets a meaning in it, now and then, that makes it seem a sadness to me.

I catch her thought so quickly; before she has fairly got it herself, she says sometimes. We do understand each other almost too well.

It is in her face, "Yes; one thing more, to fill up life, and to satisfy; if the lonely days should come."

Against this look, I thrust, the other day, a sudden word of blank diversion.

"Motherdie! What is,—mostly,—in Aunt Hetty Maria's dark closet, I wonder?"

I had been promising myself a talk about this, a long while.

"John Halliday."

I had been forgetting John Halliday these ten years. I never knew him much. He was ten years younger than I, and he came to Dearwood when he was seven or eight years old, and I was out of my childhood then, and had left off making the long play-visits in which I should have come to know and care about him. Our busy and troubled days at home — with Aunt Judith and father — began not very long after that, and I only heard a little bit here and there of what went on between Jack, as she called him, and my Aunt Hetty Maria.

He was away at school some years, and then at college; and then I know he went to Germany,—to study professionally, they said; and that he disappointed her and worried her somehow; and she was pretty strict with him, even in her way of doing every thing for him; at any rate, that they didn't get on together, and that she stopped him short at last, suddenly, and called him home; but that he went away somewhere again, soon after, and had never come back to her; and that there had been a cloud, as it were, behind her, in the lengthening years, which she was afraid to turn and look back at. Without really knowing anything, or ever before asking a word, I had felt this about Aunt Hetty Maria; so that I understood what she meant when she said, that day, — " I tell you for I know;" and I was not a bit surprised at mother's answer of the simple name: —

"John Halliday."

"What did Jack do, exactly, mother?"

"Well, it wasn't so much, perhaps, what he did do, as what he didn't; and your Aunt Hetty Maria, — well, she's as good a woman, you know, as ever grew, — except, indeed, it may be the missionaries, — but there! some people haven't any whiskers, and it's no use."

"Whiskers! mother!"

"Yes; I've thought a good many times that half the troubles in the world came of that. There's two kinds, you see, besides the cats'; outside and inside ones, — and if people don't have them, why, they're forever knocking their elbows, and breaking the noses off their pitchers, and tearing their sleeves on door-latches, and undertaking things generally that they can't get through with. Your Aunt Hetty Maria was always rather apt to try to get through holes, — and put other people through, — that she hadn't measured.

"Jack came there when his mother died, — Mr Parmenter's only, dear sister; and Aunt Hetty Maria never had a boy, and he grew up to be just like their own; but she was always strict in her ways. and more than all — if people only knew it — upon herself. She never would half 'let on,' as Emery Ann says, what she cared for anybody. And then little Mabel died, and Jack *was* all; and then she held him tighter than ever, in a queer way. She did everything, and let him have everything, really, only somehow, she took the clear comfort out of it, she was so afraid of his being spoiled. She gave him a good piece of cloth, and a long thread; only she put a pin to it instead of a needle, for fear he should make a botch. She sent him to school, and through college, and out to Europe; and he *did* pull the pin-head through, and made a pretty big hole in the cloth; he got into a way of having, and expecting, and spending, more and more; and she looking forward, all the same, to his coming back and earning his living, and putting a man's shoulder to the world's wheel. Especially after the hard times of '57 came, and so much of her money went in the great Life and Trust Company smash. Then she had to draw in; and she expected him to, right off; and then it came out that he wanted ever so much more to pay up with abroad. And then, at last, he got back; and things didn't open right out for him, and he was there at home. Idle, she thought, and not in enough hurry to bestir himself; and though she wouldn't but have done for him, she was too high-spirited for him, to like his willingness; so she had plain words with him, at last; nobody knew what; but there was more working in him of independence, may be, than showed, or than could well stand being doubted; and he spoke back, and took himself off; and she's never seen him from that day to this. Once in a while there has come a letter from somewhere, just to let her know that he was alive, and not bearing any ill-will; but no accounts of what he was doing, or word of coming home; only that in the last of the war he was a surgeon in the army under Sherman; she heard from him at Chattanooga, and he came round in the Grand March to Savannah; that was the last she knew of him; and she's proud of him, and worried out of her life about him, and turning her back all the time on something she can't bear to look at or make up her conscience about, in her dealing with him; and she's grown an old woman, and her hair and her teeth have all gone, in these ten years."

"Where was he before he went into the war?"

"There never came two letters from the same place. I suppose that was a-purpose."

XV.

INTO THE FAIRY STORY.

"Don't talk to me," mumbled Aunt Hetty Maria, "when I can't tell which is teeth, and which is bread-and-butter!"

Aunt Hetty Maria had come down again for a fortnight. To go to the dentist's, this time. I went with her, and it was pretty funny.

"I've come for the permanent set," said my aunt to Dr. T——, whom she had not seen for three years, when she took ether and pulled his hair. "I never wore the temporary ones. They were *too* temper-y. I lost all my patience with 'em. They kept me thinking of the 'wailing and gnashing,' and so of all my sins. But I've made up my mind to learn how, now."

When we asked her what for, she wouldn't tell. She was queer all through that visit. When we reminded her of what she said when she threw Dr.

T——'s first work across the room, and "took to her gums again," she only answered, "Well, I couldn't *use* 'em,— it was only looks; and who cared *then?*"

When we asked her what had made the difference and changed her mind, and who cared now, the teeth and the bread-and-butter were in the way.

When we saw that she wanted to get off, of course we didn't ask her any more. But something had evidently made a change in Aunt Hetty Maria, in more than this one thing. Every once in a while she would break out with singing to herself some line of the old song, "There's nae luck about the house," "There's nae luck at a'." She couldn't remember all the words; but the music ran in her head, she said, and so she filled it out,—between the teeth,—with any sort of syllables.

"Te i de um te diddle um
　Te diddle dum te—dair;
His very step has music in't,
　As he comes up the stair!

"De do de rol de diddle ol
　De do de rol de—dore;
Give me my cloak, I'll—du de dol,
　I'll see him come ashore!"

She kept practising what she called her "wailing and gnashing," with crackers and apples, and bits of this and that, between her visits to the dentist's and his little filings and fittings, till we thought she would ruin her appetite and digestion by the time she got the full use of her teeth; but she was in such a hurry; she "wouldn't go blundering back to Dearwood not knowing what order of natural history she belonged to, or whether her bones were outside or in. Here, there was nobody to notice; but there, there was never any knowing who might come."

She had one little double tooth on each side left out; she didn't care; her own were so for five and twenty years while the six in front were good; and she wanted to look natural. And the left large incisor must lap over its mate; her old ones did.

Something came out in Aunt Hetty Maria's face, with her new teeth, which had never been so plain there before. It was a sweetness and openness; the curve of her lips lost something that had grown set and hard in it.

I have noticed in people who have had this aid and

replenishment of art, that almost always some expression comes to light, suiting so curiously with all the other features that it is like a revelation. I know one woman who looks sly; and a man whose jaws, filled out with their new furnishing, gleam cruel, like a tiger's. I can think of others who have had disfigurement and disguise replaced with what seems more truly to belong to them, and to have been intended from the first; faces that look more gentle, generous, or delicate. And I do not believe, somehow, that anything can come out of us, by any accident, but what is in.

When Aunt Hetty Maria was packing her trunk to go away, she spoke out; her mouth was made up to it by that time.

"I've had a letter from Jack Halliday."

We might have known it was coming, even before Aunt Hetty Maria, and the teeth, and the singing. Why else did we get talking of it, that day, just a little while ago, — mother and I? Things in this world always come marked with a "to be continued." They never rise up suddenly and go right down again into their graves, like the South American mummies they tell of in the earthquake. And if they *did* do it, I don't believe it would be the last of them.

"'When the chestnuts are ripe in the old woods, and the new cider is making,'— I expect — some — to hear from him again.'"

We knew that first part was in quotation marks. She said it as we say words that have been laid by in our hearts.

"And then you have got to come up to Dearwood."

"Why, it will be almost right away, auntie."

"Yes; almost right away." It sounded like music and dancing, — the tone she spoke it in. Like the music and dancing the oldest son heard in the parable.

"Now, where *is* my second-best cap-box? Patience, won't you just see whether Emery Ann has done pressing out that piece of bobbinet? And give her this yard of wide black silk for an apron, and these two pocket-handkerchiefs."

And this was the last she would say to us then about John Halliday.

It was two weeks later when we got word and went up.

The old house was all open and sunny. Aunt Hetty Maria had delicate little lavender ribbons in her breakfast caps, and white satin ones for dinner and evening. She had left off the old black lace and purple, except when she was dusting or cooking. She looked as I remembered her fifteen years before.

It all went right through me, that morning when he came. Just as if I had been John, and Aunt Hetty Maria, and myself, all at the same identical time, and as if I had two or three different memories, and two or three different ten years were behind me. We can't help giving and taking. We can't shut ourselves up in our own separate years if we try. Then, indeed, there really *would* be only the threescore and ten, after all; and God never thought of stinting us so. He need not have made so great a world and filled it so full, if nobody was to get more out of it than that.

All John's pride and resolve, and Aunt Hetty Maria's secret tenderness and patience and pain; the work, and success, and the waiting; the mistakes and the mercy; the long silences and the shield that had been over them; the good end and the gladness; I entered into them all. They had been gathering and going on in ten years that were also of my life.

"I never meant to come back till I could pay it," — he told Aunt Hetty Maria. "It was money-pay and money-pride at first; but it changed to something different as the time went on. The thing you really cared for; I found that out; the proof that the money's worth was in me. I was only afraid — of the Boston papers. That some day I might see your name, and know it was too late."

"But what about *your* name, Jack? Did you think I wouldn't look for that?"

"My name has been in the papers, now and then, I guess. Most men's have, of late years. But I cut the head and tail off, and threw them in the fire, in the first place; as the White Cat did in the fairy story, when she wanted to be turned into something better," Jack answered, lightly.

When he said that, I jumped right off my chair. As true as I live, it never came into my head before. I hadn't remembered it for years and years; but now it flashed across me, — the boy's long name as I had heard it some time when he first came to Uncle Parmenter's.

John Robert Haile Halliday.

"What's that for, Patience?" said John, as I sat down again.

"I don't think it was a good plan. Or a right plan," said I, catching my breath from my surprise, and speaking quite decided and resentful. "What if it didn't turn out so wonderfully much better, after all, and the head and tail had to be raked out of the ashes and tacked on again? Or if some people, — some*body*, — had come to like the middle part best? As they couldn't ever, perhaps, like the rest of it, or any name, again? I think it was too bad upon them!"

John came right over to me where I sat, and deliberately pinched me. So that nobody else could see, however.

"Patience Strong! You're rather confused in your analogy, but — you know a good deal too much!" he whispered.

Everybody knew it pretty soon, though. It was a turn-outing; such as they pretend to keep for stories; but such as happens every day in the life that stories are made up out of. And I had been in every bit of it; first one part and then another. Whose story was it, I should like to know, more than mine; or half so much, — seeing that *they* couldn't possibly be on both sides of themselves!

It was a little hard for Aunt Hetty Maria at the very first, to be sure; just as if she had only got him back to give him right away again; but almost before she knew it, she was taking Rose straight into her heart and home, planning which rooms would do for her, and thinking whether she had better put up red curtains or white ones in the long chamber; and that " it would have to be before the dreary weather came, — she couldn't bear to think of a wedding in November; — mightn't we make it out for the thirtieth? There was something so glad about October; the very sound of it was yellow and bright, like fruits and sunshine and tingling juices and clear, frosty air."

All this, taking it for granted that Dearwood should be their first home; that she had a right to them both. All talked over, again and again, while Dr. John was down at M—— making " head and tail " of it as best he could, with the Nobles.

And then he brought Rose up for a three days' visit to his mother; and she, in her own dear little way, settled everything as she chose.

" Let us come back and build our own nest, with you to help us, please," she said to Aunt Hetty Maria, when Jack was out of the room. " Don't you tire yourself all out alone, and take away all the good of it. You see we should have nothing to do but to sit right down in a finished place, and that's always disappointing. People that do the making ready, put thoughts and thoughts into it, one after another, with every little fixing and touching; and then, just in a minute, the folks that come are shown in, and it's all over. Let's have the thoughts and the comfort together, please."

And so it was the nicest nest-building that ever was. We were all there, and there was plenty of room for us all, beside the long chamber and the "little bay," that we were fixing up.

And they had been married a fortnight, and Rose could speak her mind, and say how she wanted things; and John Halliday's books and pictures, and Rose's piano and plants and wedding presents had all come; and we were nailing, and hanging, and consulting, and placing; and nobody did anything that all the rest didn't stand round and admire. And Hannah Ferson — Aunt Hetty Maria's Hannah — whenever she came to look, said it was "so pleasant and folksy!" And Aunt Hetty Maria herself was everywhere; and everybody was calling her from everywhere else, to ask her this or show her that.

"Auntie!"

"Mother!"

"Hetty Maria!"

"Mis' Parmenter!"

came from upstairs, downstairs, and the lady's chamber.

"Here I am, — all four of me!" she would call back. And in a minute, all four of her would be there.

"She was just the spryest!" old Mrs. Whitgift said, making the little entry carpet, and being stepped over twenty times a day.

"Nobody gave me a silver pitchfork, after all," said Rose Halliday, up at the top of a flight of steps, hanging a basket, and looking for scissors to cut the cord.

Jack made a stride across the room to where they lay, and a long arm up to her to give them.

"And I don't know that I really see the need," she added, "if this is to last."

I guess it will last, — all the help and comfort John Halliday can give her, — to the end of his life.

I have had the beauty of it, — I who never was married, or like to be; and it makes my heart warm.

And mother and I are going home again, now.

XVI.

WITH THE SUNDAY STRAYS.

It is strange how one little glimpse, one little taste, — of another person's living or gladness, — stays by you, and opens the door toward all the rest. Every morning, now, when the north-west air is crisp with mountain frosts, and the smell of ripeness comes with every stir, and the sun-glory is keen in the clean-swept atmosphere, and the crown of the year's joy lies upon the earth, I think, the first thing, of the pleasantness up there at Dearwood; of the new, bright home there; or, rather, of the fresh, beautiful soul in the old. Of John and Rose standing always on the morning-threshold, looking into the years together, as we look into the hours when the day is prime; of the cosey breakfast, and the after-breakfast settling; of Rose with her work-basket in her window among her plants; of Doctor Halliday reading; of

Aunt Hetty Maria looking in every little while, as she goes up and down, upon this new acquisition of hers of young, beautiful life; continually wanting fresh little views of it, as we do of pretty and comfortable things we have just got and brought home.

When the night draws in, and the fire is cheerful, and the winter-lamp is lighted that has been set by through the warm, twilighted evenings, and all the comfort that has ever been in one's life, or that one has read of, seems to wrap itself around one in a delicious fulness, — then again I think of Dearwood, and of all the long, happy winter that is before them there; before them to whom a single hour together was but a little while ago so much. Of the pretty worsted work Rose meant to do, that she never had had time for in her busy, careful life at home; of Aunt Hetty Maria knitting, and John drawing, or wood-turning, — for he does all sorts of charming, ingenious things, — and of all the pleasant choice of thought, and talk, and occupation, which that free time gives when there are no old things to mend, no hurry of providing, no anxious complications to unravel, such as come with the living on,—but all is new and plentiful, and smooth with the smoothness of that which is unbegun.

Why, it is beautiful just to know of it! And they, after all, can't *more* than know of it themselves. Possession is only intimacy of knowledge. The good and the beauty of it is the *fact* in God's world. I think that is the blessedness that foretells itself in the "knowing as we are known." Then everybody's joy will be fully ours. Then they shall sit down by fifties and by hundreds, and one bread shall be given to all; and of the fragments that remain shall be taken up baskets and baskets full; and worlds, perhaps, shall be fed with the crumbs that fall from the Master's table.

But the worst of it is, that, if I don't look out, I shan't do my own living. That is the reason why we may, now, see only in part. It is so easy to abide in that love which is only loving imagination; the love of act may be waiting, meanwhile, in our own unlived days.

My days ought to be very full this winter; so much crowds upon me to do and to care for.

Now that I have found out I can paint, I think of so many people who can't buy pictures that I might make them for. I gave Mrs. Shreve a maple branch crossed by a stem of sumach. She hung it over her mantel, and said it was as good as a fire. I must do something for Seelie Rubb. And I want to copy the Mater Admirabilis, with the lily and the distaff, for my dear little mother, at Christmas time.

Besides that, the new horse-railroad is opened at last, as far as Hibben's Lane. Only five minutes' walk from our door. Why, we are almost city people! But mother and I don't go in much. At first I thought we shouldn't be much concerned. I didn't worry about the Sunday people, and the fruit-trees, and the gardens, as some of the neighbors did. In fact, I have had so many other things to take up my mind, that I really thought very little about it, until all at once when we got home from Dearwood, we found that the cars were to run, and that we were to be Metropolitans the very next Monday. Things always do get finished up, or broken off, or changed somehow, while you're gone.

It has come to me since — the force of it — talking with Seelie Rubb. She was here one day last week, to cut my new brown empress cloth. It's just — more outings; these very Sunday outings.

"I'm so glad," Seelie said, "of these new horse-cars. Susan came out last Sunday, with her husband and two of her children, to drink tea. The other two are coming next time. Why, it seemed almost like Thanksgiving. Mother said she didn't know as she should ever have used her best cups and saucers again — they'd been put away so long. They're real, beautiful china, Miss Patience; and the plates; there's only seven left of *them*, but they've each got a separate figure. There's currants on one, and strawberries on another, and cherries, and plums, and peaches, and grapes, and a cut pomegranate; and with every fruit there's a little blossom of its own dropped on one side. Mother says it always makes her feel *like people* again to set them out."

Seelie set up the shoulder-puff of my sleeve half an inch higher, as she spoke, giving an air, I suppose, more "like people" to my plain, winter dress, than it might have had but for the little accompanying puff and set-up of her spirits, as she told about the plates.

"That isn't too high, is it?" I asked, a little anxiously.

"Oh, dear, no, miss; the higher and squarer the better, now. Why, they actually put little crutches under their shoulders, somehow, they say, to raise them up. And what with the buckram fronts, and the panniers behind, and other things that they just whisper about,— why, besides needing to be a qualified architect and engineer before you can be a real dress-maker, I aint truly sure, sometimes, that it isn't a downright wickedness altogether!"

"People talk," said I, " about *Boston* not being finished. I wonder if the *women* ever will be. They've been added on to and taken off from, and lengthened out and cut short, and humped up and flattened down, and I don't know how many different things, since I can remember. I wonder if they'll ever find out what is just right and prettiest, and stop there and be comfortable."

"No, in*deed*," said Seelie Rubb, with a simple little consternation in her voice at such a foolish looking for.

"Do you know, Seelie," I said, soberly, "that when I hear these things, I feel as if I saw the 'abomination of desolation standing in the holy place'? And I can seem to understand the 'woe' to those who shall be mothers 'in those days!'"

"It is pretty bad, Miss Patience," little Seelie repeated, shaking her head. "And it does make me feel wicked, learning to make a trade of it. Why, it isn't hardly much better, seems to me,— some of it,— than selling liquor to the men!"

"Only you work for the plain people, Seelie; it doesn't touch your conscience quite so closely. And you don't *contrive* the fashions, you know, to lead the silly women captive."

"Why, Miss Patience, there *aren't* any plain people! The delaines and the alpacas have to be humped up and flounced out, just as much as the silks and the poplins. And there's just where the wickedness comes in — or out, at least. It isn't so much for the rich women, who only drive to the dress maker's, and give their orders; but I know lots of mothers and girls who have to spend all their time and their brains on the home-made things, and more money, besides, than they've any business to. A merino gown, or a poplin-alpaca, isn't much; but by the time you've got the buttons, and the ribbons, and the braid, and the haircloth, and have spent a week putting it together, it gives you a feeling in the pit of your stomach as if you'd got a broken commandment there."

"But about your sister, and the horse-railroad. How nice it is, — this coming out to Sunday home-teas, — for the city people!"

"Why, you don't know!" said Seelie. "I go down to church in the car, sometimes, now, it's such a long walk; and the fathers and mothers, and little children that get in and out, with their hands full and hearts full of the country, just this once a week, — it's beautiful! It makes me think of the Lord walking in the corn-fields. And it's true for more than the walking, too, I'm afraid. I guess the poor things are pretty well a-hungered, some of them, before they get back. They don't all have home-teas to come to."

"They ought to, Seelie, somehow!"

That was my first thought about it; and it stayed by, although I had to turn it over awhile before I could quite see the New Testament part without the queerness.

I *don't* want to be crazy-queer, about anything; and I know it's no use to expect to provide for all the Sunday strays, and that it wouldn't always do if you could; but then to think of the young fathers and mothers,— week-workers,— bringing out the little children into the blessed country on the day of the Son of Man, and going back, any of them, worn and hungry! *He* always had compassion on the multitudes, and cared lest, possibly, there might any faint by the way. If we could get out of this world into the nearest edge of the heavenly places, once in a while, would the angels shut their doors, I wonder? Wouldn't they rather take us in and feed us with the bread of the kingdom? I think we should look for them to do so, and that our idea of the heaven we may go into by and by, is, first of all, of somebody coming to meet us.

I thought and thought, till I felt there was surely something, in the way of a loaf, for me to do. And that was the beginning.

Mother and I talked it over. And so, Saturday, we baked a basket of crisp gingerbread and fried a panful of doughnuts, and Sunday morning we set out a pitcher of milk from the milking. And then we were all ready; if the little children did come along.

Then, being all ready, I began to be afraid they wouldn't come, — our way. So, about three o'clock, I said to mother : —

" Motherdie! I believe I'll put on my hat and shawl, and walk down toward the head of the lane, and see what I can see."

And mother laid her spectacles down on the window-sill, and smoothed out her lap, saying : —

"So I would. They might turn off the other road, by the brook; and that would be a pity, seeing the doughnuts and the gingerbread are up here; besides the lane, that of course they wouldn't know of"

We had really began to expect some special " they."

It was a lovely late autumn day. It seemed as if the sun had done his summer work, and the spare fragments of his glory were flung down upon us for pure joy. As if human creatures might have them all, now that the grain was ripe and the grass gone, and the fruit mellow. It was like " after the party."

I met them just there, by the brook; or rather I saw them coming, and managed that they should overtake me with my face toward home, as I stood and picked some bits of bright leaves out of the hedge.

They came up chattering, — the little ones. I had been puzzling what I could say if they didn't take our road; indeed, what I could exactly say if they did. But you always see as you come to it.

" Let's go this way," says the biggest girl. " Down here, where this pretty water goes."

" No," says the boy, sturdily. " I don't care for the water. I saw a squirrel up here on the wall. I want to see where *he* goes to."

" It's quieter this way," suggests the man.

" And sunnier this," replies the woman.

"Well, mother, what do you say? Say quick!"

These last were evidently words of habit with the husband, — spoken always in that smiling way and cheery tone, — meaning: —

"All you have to do is to settle your own wish. My way's yours. And I'm not in the least bit of a hurry. So — say quick!"

I took it to myself; feeling in such a hurry lest they should choose the other road.

So I "said quick" just what came into my head.

"If you want to take the children a pleasant walk, ma'am, I can show you a beautiful green lane up here a little way that leads down into the woods."

"Oh, thank you! Come, James, we'll go this way, if this lady is so kind."

So we walked on together, and mother, looking out of her window, saw me coming up, just as if I had been to meet Eliphalet's folks down at the cars. I almost caught myself calling up to her, — "Yes, they've come!" They were so exactly the very people we had been looking for.

Of course I didn't suppose they were hungry yet,

and I couldn't do everything all at once. I showed them down the green lane, and left them to find their own way and their own happiness by themselves; only I did just bethink myself to turn back and say to the elder girl, lest they should happen to get out by the turnpike, and so round: —

"Come back this way, dear, and stop a minute, and I will give you some flowers."

So we were sure of our company now, mother and I; and we went and sugared a plate of doughnuts, and had mugs handy for the children; and then I sat down again and went on reading to her out of the "Schönberg-Cotta Family."

XVII.

INTO OTHER PEOPLE'S BUSINESS.

So that began it. And now, as I said, I have plenty to plan and to do. Because, although the pleasant autumn weather is soon over, and the winter-time is no time for Sunday-outings, yet I know how it will be when the spring comes; and how Fast Day, and May Day, and every day that they can get, will be bringing them, — those that I have got acquainted with (and it is wonderful how one gets on in any particular world of people when one once begins with one or two), and many more.

And they shall all be welcome. We shall have to bake bigger baskets of gingerbread, and fry huger pans of doughnuts, and keep out whole bowls of milk; but there shall not one of them go by our door wishful or weary.

And it gives the chance for other things. One doing

lights the way to the next. All the little paths and aisles toward the light of the Great Love open into each other.

There are books and pictures and things to look at, for the fathers and mothers, and the little children. Books to lend too; they like so to take something home. So I have got plain-bound copies, and copies second-hand, nicely covered, — quite a bookshelf full, — of pleasant, useful reading, on purpose; and it is nice to have plenty of money to do this with so comfortably. I buy cheaply, and make the most; for I like to keep the feeling of being rich behind my doing, as long as I can. Some things must cost; the stereoscopic views, for instance. I have two glasses, and a great many pictures; I can never have too many of these. Why, when they get out here, — these friends of mine, — which is as far as they will ever get, most of them, in point of fact, — I can take them right on into all the beautiful unknown places of the wide world. Into the Alp-heights, and the Yo-Semite; to Niagara and Trenton and Mount Washington; up the Saguenay and the Mississippi; among the Dalles of the St. Croix and to the falls of the Minnehaha. These are the people that ought to go in this way. What a shame it would be to keep such wonderful glimpses in rich parlors and libraries only; for people who can go far and wide, if they choose, among the realities!

Of them all, that which gives most awe and pleasure is the moon-picture. The great telescopic moon, hanging in black space, with its jagged mountains catching the beams of the eternal sun, and flinging down the self-same actual points of light that have so rested there, on the little card held up to it for its portrait two hundred and forty thousand miles away.

The great Nothing that it is in! The upholding of its separate round mass! The present hand of God, more truly recognized because no hold is seen! Foundationless! If the old Eastern tradition had any truth, — if the earth were a flat plain and seemed to rest on anything; if its great pillars stood upon an elephant, and the elephant upon a tortoise, and the tortoise on something untraceable in depth, but not beyond conception, — where would be our thought of the environing spirit? This wonderful, awful *floating* of everything, from the sun-globes to the meanest atoms,— this utter separateness,— it is by this we get an inmost notion of that rest, that reliance, that nearness, that strength, in which we lie!

It comes into their faces, every one,— more or less dimly or consciously,— as they look at this moon-picture. I need not say a syllable, I know. It will tell it to them for itself. The word it speaks will bury itself in their souls; a seed to grow up into the grandest, holiest knowledge.

It is something to minister such sacraments as these.

"It is all very well," Emery Ann says, "with the decent mechanic people. But how will you do when the ragged boys and the coarse men get wind of it and come along?"

"I suppose I shall think when the time comes," I answered. "And if they are *too* coarse, I dare say nothing will drive them away sooner than politeness."

"There's something in that," said Emery Ann. "My sister Loviny used to tell her little boy,— 'Don't come into the parlor unless you can be polite.' So one day he stood in the doorway when she had company 'Why don't you come in, Horatio, and take off your cap?' says Loviny. 'I don't feel as if I wanted to be polite,' says he, and cleared. It don't alwers take a perleece officer to keep folks out from where they aint fit,—not even, forzino, out of heaven."

Mother says she's " proper glad " we thought of it Dear mother! What shall we do when the quaint old people are all gone, and the quaint old words are all used up? They are a part of speech by themselves; not common, not ill-bred, nor *anything* like modern slang; but full of pure meaning and time-flavor. The old Puritans sent them down to us, many of them; this, certainly. They were so self-contained; and words were so chastened in their using. Nobody was ever *extravagantly* glad; nothing was ever *excessively* pleasant; only " properly " so. Yet the sober word meant all that they could say, as much as our words do; and the meaning grew more and more, as they crowded all their feeling into it, until the very term of moderation and restraint came to have a most lip-smacking sound of the superlative.

Sometimes I think I get more out of other people than is fair; I have grown so into the way of putting myself in their places, and feeling just how things must seem to them. It is almost like reading their letters, or listening at their doors. I wonder if it's old maids' way; and if that is how we get such a character; because we must needs borrow so much? I wonder if it is the essence of prying and gossiping?

I think the difference must be in the point of view. If you stand outside, and peer and pick and criticise, — if you look for what had better not be, — then I'm sure choking in the sea isn't a bit too bad for such a haunting and possessing; but if you go right down into their hearts, and feel their joys and troubles with them, — I think that is even what our Lord himself did, and how he helped them, and "bore" their sorrows and iniquities, and gave them of his peace.

I try to have it so. For my imagination — whatever that is, and I think it is the power that goes out of us into spiritual places, gathering realities — *will* reach forth and lay hold of what is not, altogether, my very own.

l g;, here and there, in this fashion. To Dearwood, as I was saying; and lately, very much, just in this way, to Mrs. Shreve's.

She has had a piece of good fortune. She has had some money left her. Money that she never expected or heard of. "Things are never done happening, in this world," Emery Ann says. "Everything can wait, but chickens and children."

Late in life, after many pinches and worries, it has come to her. Not an enormous fortune; but that large "enough" to her quiet wants, that sets her heart at rest.

And it is so pleasant to feel how it is with her. And she shows it so simply. Not by any airs or pretences, — no, indeed! Only by breathing free; as if some band were loosened that had drawn tight around her life.

She makes half-a-dozen new night-gowns; "in case of sickness," she says, — "it is good to have a store," — and I know, with the high price of cotton, she did not have more than two new ones together, for many a year; and she sends by me to buy Coventry ruffling, by the piece, for the necks and bands. She gets nice, new napkins, — I marked them for her with an old English S in indelible ink, — and she hires a woman by the day to help her girl with the washing, or when there is extra scrubbing to do. She has let Dick go to a tailor, and the world is thereby a shade brighter all over to the boy. She has a fire and a large lamp in the best room, of evenings, when he comes home; and when mother and I go over, neighboring, the whole house looks as if it were always so, and could be as well as not. Nothing is very strange or new; only safe and sure and hearty. When a thing breaks, she says "Never mind!" not keeping the "mind" all to herself, with a pain, like a secret returning echo. I think she can't help a sort of satisfaction, now and again, in a little loss or a giving out; knowing that the replacing is no longer a taking from one thing to make good another.

The way it happened was this.

I know that if I were putting together a story, — for the sake of the story, — which I never meant to do, and never could have done in all my life, — the way it happened ought to have come first; indeed everything ought to have come first, except the very thing that I was driving at. Not by any means with A, B, and C regularity either; I know better than that, too; you must " say it, skipping about; " I have not read the new style of novel and magazine writing unobservantly. You must dip first into a little bit of the end; then plunge into the middle, talking about people and places and things, as if everybody had been regularly introduced, and then gradually, by little dashes and allusions, catchings up and hitchings on, get the antecedents and the connections together, with the help of the clever reader, — and nobody else has any business with modern literature, — in a manner equally creditable to his sagacity and your own ingenuity.

But, as I am not writing a story, — only putting down things and thoughts as they come to me, in a very plain, small, every-day living, — I put down first what interests me most, — dear Mrs. Shreve's long breath.

The way it happened, then, was this: —

I was looking out of my window one day, when I saw a very queer little man getting out of a very queer little chaise, at Mrs. Shreve's door.

The man was short and thin; the chaise was tall and thin; and the horse was a roan, chunky and low; so low that he made me think of a little spotted dog, trained to run between the wheels, and that the real horse must be somewhere, invisibly, beyond, or round the corner.

The man had wiry little legs, and a round ball of a head, and he wore the roundest of brown felt hats; and his thick, short sack-coat, also brown, set out round his body so as to complete another ridiculous notion that came into my head, that he was like an unfinished piece of knitting-work; the needles stuck into the ball at one end, and the piece of web rounding out between. And his name was according to my fancy, and bore it out curiously, as I learned afterwards. It was Mr. Knott Webber, the keen little Boston lawyer.

A certain client of his — Aaron Eachfield — had just died.

Some years ago, this Aaron Eachfield, a master mechanic, came into his office, for the first time, in company with Richard Shreve, whose widow, — as he said at this point of the interview which Mrs. Shreve mostly repeated to me, word for word, here and there, from time to time afterward, quite in the approved constructive style I was just speaking of, and which I, with the due cleverness, patched and pieced together, till I have got the whole incident very clearly and prettily in my head, — whose widow, he said, he believed he had now the pleasure of addressing.

Mr. Shreve had been in a large way of business, and had gone into many building speculations. These it was that ruined him, as to money's worth, — finally; but meanwhile, he had put work and money in others' way, and had built up many a modest little fortune, although failing, at last, of his own. I believe there are books somewhere, on which there will be found records that make him a heavy stockholder in a kind of Mutual Company whose dividends pay largest and best after all earthly accounts are closed.

"I've brought you a man, Mr. Webber," said Mr.

Shreve to his lawyer, "who wants somebody to draw up his will. My friend, Mr. Aaron Eachfield; my friend, Mr. Knott Webber. And now, as I have an important appointment in a quarter of an hour, I'll leave you to get better acquainted without me."

And that was the last Richard Shreve ever knew of the business.

Aaron Eachfield turned round to the lawyer.

"Yes, sir. I've laid up a snug little property, of some thirty thousand dollars. And that man, sir, who's just gone out, is the man that put me in the way of it. I may say it's his gift. For a gift comes down, sir, through many hands; and in every one it's as real a giving, as though God Almighty weren't at one end, and a fellow's own hard work at the other. But that's taking up your time; I beg your pardon. What I want, is a will, right and tight; disposing of this said thirty thousand dollars in two equal halves. One to my wife, Rebecca Eachfield, and I'm sorry to say I haven't seen her for as many years as I've given her thousands, and them more, I'm afraid, than'll do her any real good. Then, provided I leave no child or child's child, — and the only one there is isn't likely to marry or to outlive me, poor thing, — the other half to Richard Shreve, Esquire, or his widow, or his oldest child, whichever stands to represent him, if so be, after I'm gone. And that being the whole of it, I don't know as I need to bother you much longer now. When it's done, I'll come and sign."

And the little lawyer having unravelled himself of this, held out his hand, and shook Mrs. Shreve's warmly, and told her he was glad in his soul to have to come and tell her of it.

"For Aaron Eachfield was a grand good fellow; and Richard Shreve, — well, you know, ma'am, what he was; and it's good money that comes through such men's fingers; and I wish you well of it; *well* of it ma'am; in my soul I do!"

After that, I saw the rest of it; the little knitting-work man sticking his brown ball (apparently) on its pins again, and rolling himself up as if he had done his stent for that time, and getting into his tall chaise again, and rattling away with the little roan horse trotting underneath.

And so that night, happening in, I saw that Mrs. Shreve was rather nervous; and, lighting her lamp, and putting the globe on, she let it slip, and broke it into fifty pieces against the stove-foot; upon which, while I picked up the scraps of glass, she sat down and burst out crying.

I knew she couldn't well spare the dollar it would take to buy another; but I was afraid, for her giving way like this, which wasn't usual to her, that the knitting-work man must have brought some botch or other to worry her; and I began to be quite angry with him in my heart, and to feel as if I should like to pull out all his stitches.

And then, when she got over it a little, she told me not to mind; what made her cry was, that it was no kind of matter; that she could get as many lamp-shades as she liked; and that nobody had ever had such a husband; and that it would be an ache in her heart all her life that she'd never seen Aaron Eachfield, to tell him what she thought of him, and to say God bless him!

And if that wasn't beginning in the right modern

style to tell a story, I should like to know what would have been!

So first and last, between us, it's all the same. If any one likes it better so, they can begin at this end and read it again, backward. Anyhow, there's a new chamber firelighted and warm in my heart; a new place to go into and be glad in; every time I think of Mrs. Shreve and her lamp-shades, and her bonnets, and her table-cloths, and her night-gowns, and all the little things that used to fret and trouble her, and that now she can be so easy about.

And, as Emery Ann says, — We can all wait our turn; things are never done happening; everybody can be patient but children and chickens.

XVIII.

INTO THE MIDNIGHT.

WEEKS ago, I wrote those last words.

How can I bear to put it down here, — that which came after?

The pleasant heart-chambers are all shut up.

God has called me out — into the darkness. I grope and grope, reaching after my life that is taken away from me, and set so far onward.

I know that it is the *evening* and the morning that are the day; I know the morning is beyond; but the midnight is heavy upon me.

O mother! my dear, dear little mother!

XIX.

INTO THE DAY-GLEAM.

HER empty chair is before my eyes.

The little stand is there, and the work-basket; and her spectacles are lying on the window-ledge.

Nobody touches them but me, and I place them every morning as she did. I do not let the dust lie on them, but I will never put them away.

Yet it is not the chair, nor any place, that held her.

When she was there, to my sight, it was not all of her. It was only the sign of her. Her real presence was in all the room, — in all the house. In all the world, lighting it up for me.

Is it different now because the sign is set elsewhere in another chamber, higher up? When I was down stairs and she above, the house was no less full of her. When I went miles away my life was no less full of her.

I am coming to think of it so. I am coming,

through days and nights of pain, to the beginning of the sun-break. Not out into darkness, but out into the breadth and glory of the many mansions, has the Good Father called my soul.

When I think how it has been between us,—how the blue of the morning, and the sweetness of the summer, and the little pleasantness of home, and the thought that from anywhere came to touch us both, were the things that held us really close, and that our hearts met in,—I know that the bodily presence was not much,—was not our living. And that our real life can *not* be broken.

I set her place straight, and put the little things about, there in the window, and make up the dear look of the pleasant day we are to have together; and the same love is in it that was in it then; and so the soul is in it; and so the pleasant day *must be*, and is.

Does not she know? How did she know it then?

It was not in the table, nor the chair, nor the book, nor the basket; only that our thought met in these,— in that which was within them, rather, and behind the signs.

It is only that,—that she has gone *behind the signs*.

Into the very peace of the blue morning, into the very rest of the tender twilight, into the very joy of the new-springing thought that wants and waits not words; into the continual promise and forelooking of the pleasant day that is always just begun.

When these things touch me, through the types, she is in them with me, without the types. Just as she was before. She has entered the within. The within that is also the beyond, and the unbound.

Out, into the wider life,—into the spiritual places. Is this whither He would lead me now, by her dear drawing and guidance? Then ought I to be glad; gladder than in any other leading He has ever given.

Only, the pain and the strain! The reaching forth one's hands, with the clog of the flesh upon them, to lay hold of things in that world the things of which may neither be touched nor handled!

This blind walking in the midst of glory! I know that it is here, and close; and to her it is manifest. But I am as the beggar crying by the wayside, among the crowds that looked upon the face of the Lord,—

feeling only that he is here, and that the great multitude is about him,— crying only "Have mercy on me, that I may receive my sight!"

Yet, when my heart is warm, I know, as the blind know, that I am in the sunshine that I cannot see.

I had a dream of her.

It seemed to me that I had work in my hand; large work,— sewing; and that I went down the garden with it alone. I came to a wall— a wall freshly built, — that stopped me. I wondered, — and then I remembered. "The sepulchre! In my garden, also, there is a new tomb, now!"

When, behold, in the seeming sepulchre, a door; which, when I opened, showed me a fair room, full of sunshine; and in the sunshine, as if she were the heart of it, she sat. And she had work in her hand, like mine; only it was finished. And she spoke in the dear old tone, and the light was all around her, and in her look.

"Childie! Come to sit and work with me? That is good. Sit here, where it is warm and pleasant:

sew your seam, while I pick out the basting-threads from this of mine."

And I never felt her company so dear and sweet, in all my waking life, as I felt it in that moment of my dream.

Words woke me, that were spoken in the spirit. "I am the Door; by Me ye shall go in and out." And the rest of it came after; the word of my vision.

Motherdie! I *will* bring my work in my hand, and sit with you in the sunshine. I will patiently sew my seam of life that is not yet ended, while you draw out the earth-threads from your beautiful finished garment. And all the same, our labor is one, as it was before.

I am glad you can draw out the threads, motherdie! the threads of the seam that I have still to do; and I am glad, and I know, that you still work on somehow beside me. I am glad of the sunny mansion, and of the door that opens easily and gently inward. Close by,—out of the garden,—out of the nearest pleasantness of visible things!

Everybody thought, at first, that I would go away from here. Why, where should I go? If this were lonely, what would the wide world be, where she never was? And if this were her home, where her spirit clung so long, where else should I find the sweet haunting of her life and love, that are the only presence, let the body be laid down as it may?

No; I shall stay here. If I went away, I must needs come back, haunting, too. And I feel as if I should meet, in the spirit, a tender reproach, — a sigh of "how could you?" through the dear, old, forsaken rooms.

At first I was afraid that I should not have Emery Ann. She, too, had made up her mind for me, that I must needs go; and her brother had written to her, again and again, from away down East, at Skowhegan, that he wanted her there to keep his house.

So there came to be so much said and thought about it before she realized that I would still certainly want her here, that it divided her mind. She felt, she said, "as if she had actually moved, and the thing was now to come back again." I wanted her to take her free choice, and I told her to think it over as long as she liked.

That means, keep moving. Why, I shall be all ore out, going back and forrard in my mind; and good for nothing for either of you by then I stop. I tell you, Miss Patience, you don't know what an awful waggle a settled kind of a mind gets into, when once it *is* upsot!"

So poor Emery Ann laid awake nights, and came down with her eyes all dropped in, in the morning, and brought in breakfast like an Affery Flintwinch in a dream.

She looked sometimes as if she wanted me to question her, to get a decision out of her that she was quite beyond producing for herself.

"Well?" said I, one morning, more as an answer to her own eyes than as an inquiry.

"Well," she replied; as if the forced decision were coming, and glad too, — and then suddenly caught herself back into the debatable ground again. She set down the tray, and lifted up her hand, moving her thumb to and fro, as the children do in the game of "Simon."

"Well, ma'am, — Simon says — Wigwag!"

And every morning after that, for about a week, she would set down the tray without a word, and lift up her hand, and make the sign.

But at last she came in with a brighter face than she had worn since — since the change and shadow fell; and when she had emptied her hands of their burden, she made a great sweep in the air and brought her right thumb downward upon the table, planting it there as if she stamped some solemn and irrevocable seal.

"Simon says — DOWN, ma'am!"

And I believe it is down, now, for as long as we both shall live.

I asked her how it had come about.

"Well, ma'am, I've been tossed by the winds, and in jeopardy. But the Lord has kept me in one mind now, — for I just left it all to him when I found I couldn't stay there a minute myself, — for twenty-four hours together; and so he's brought me to land. I can tell a sign when it does come, besides its being a thankful deliverance."

I believe nothing lifts us so far forward as pain and hardness.

I do not think, as I sometimes have thought and been afraid, that they, in the heaven-peace and freedom, will go on so fast beyond us as to go *away*. I think that we who stay and *bear*, are climbing by rough, grand steps to as beautiful a height. And that they must see it so; as we see hard lives and great anguishes here, and behold them with a reverence.

I believe the earth life *is* grand; almost grander than the first heaven of rest it reaches to. I think the Father's angels must have looked with a more worshipping awe on the Son of Man in the glory of his suffering, than in the glory of his power.

It can only be that it is one same world, where one same work of love and faith is done under different conditions. And I can think, somehow, of how it may be, and of things it is like.

The man, for instance, grapples numbers in his brain, and sum and relation are beautiful abstract truths; abstract, but real; the *more* real; and he feels that he gets *hold* of them somehow. The little child slides colored balls on wires, and cannot go beyond his sight. Yet they are both reaching into the same realm, and touch, mentally, the same things.

We work in the spiritual relations by signs. The angels work in the inner things themselves. And these inner things are not in one corner of the universe and their signs in another. I believe it is one great *Here*.

I think of it when I walk in the streets of the wonderful, busy city. I think of what is there beside the stones and the buildings. Of what they stand for, or else they could not stand at all; of the real grandness and strength; of the thought-work and living energies, and of the needs and loves out of which these things grow; and I think that behind the things which we "behold," and of which, some day, perhaps, "there shall not be one stone left upon another," there is something immortal which shall not pass away; some word of God; and that, in the midst, the spirits of God are walking with us even now.

Of God,—or of evil; for the kingdoms may be growing together,—their very stones interlocked and cemented; yet in the unseen, knowing each other not. Divided by the great gulf which is not depth or distance, only utter unrelation; as there are powers and properties in nature that coexist, yet never touch or recognize or invade each other, because they have no common end or tending.

I think of it in the simplest things of every day and of our doing; as our tastes develop and our life expresses itself; as we make about us the look that we love best; that we are building, so, the very home in the heavens, that is now, and shall be.

Perhaps I cannot so much as put a flower in a vase, or hang a picture on the wall, or make anything sweet and clean and let the sunshine in upon it, without putting what the flower and the picture and the sunlighted purity *mean* into the unseen mansion that is here, and is waiting.

It always seems as if one did more than the mere thing. If I move about a little furniture, and make some room that I had not before, the range and spaciousness are not just exactly the feet that I have gained, but a grand, indefinite opening. It is an idea of latitude that is as good to me, and signifies as much, as any breadth of emptiness that could be built around with walls.

Children see this poetry of things, — which is their spirit, — always. The high, broad steps or stairs they always like to play on are more to them than a mere way of getting up. The little cricket in the corner, the nice corner itself, the seat in the apple-tree, — these things to the child have life and importance, because the child does "always behold" the inward of things. Growing older, we forget; or greater things displace these little ones; we can sit anywhere; yet we do like our corner still. Enough lingers with us to keep the soul of the home-idea; and we go on gathering round it the body which fits and sets forth the spirit. We are "building better than we know."

I think, — I am sure, — motherdie! that we have built together. That you are in it with me, still; the home that this is the sign and the outshowing of; the home that is not "very far off."

XX.

INTO THE MORNING.

The sunshine among my flowers, to-day, made me so glad! It came in among them from away through the far heaven, and touched every little stem and leaf with a thread, a pulse, of the glory that is also at the same moment, unbroken, in the deep heart of the Sun!

It tells so much. Everything is such a showing. When we begin to look at it so, all life is such a divine parable. And the things of this world are what we cannot possibly stop in; but ways out; every way, into the everlasting life.

Ways out! That was what I began, in my simpleness, to write about, not knowing how far it would take me, or how much I was meaning in the little things that I was trying to say.

I found out what my " outings " were, that reached,

by insight, or imagination, or sympathy, or little doings of some sort of kindness, into life and range beyond my own little quietness and abiding.

I found so many doors stood open; that that which seemed the very stop and closure was only a gate that swung on easy, delicate hinges, to let me through into a wider place.

But I hardly knew how it was all one,— the nearest and the farthest. I hardly thought what narrowing of loss and pain it would be that should come and shut me in for a season, only to broaden out — as it is broadening — into glimpses of that life our living all takes hold of, and all our loving is projected into; of that kingdom, the gates of which are never shut at all by day; and, as to the night-time, there is no night there!

This is the beautiful Easter-time.

Yesterday there were flowers in the church; sweet spring flowers, white and tender, like new-born hopes; and bright, fresh, living green.

To-day, motherdie, there are flowers in your window, — Easter flowers; white and purple crocuses and snowdrops. You love the crocus, mother! You used to say it was "such a comforting little flower; it came before you expected it." So I put them there to-day; and the comfort looks out at me from their delicate faces.

The house is pleasant, mother!

The winter is gone; and in the winter-time I found new ways of making pleasantness, — for you and me! For you are in it all, and it is for your sake. I learn so the deep sweetness Christ meant for us, when he bade us do for his sake!

We are not lonely here. *You* never were lonely; and I would not let any dreariness come down about your home.

When Emery Ann made up her mind — her good, kind, faithful mind — to stay by me, — by us, mother! she had a hard indecision to win through.

"For you see," she said, "the main thing is, that now Matilda is going to be married, ma was talkin' some of breakin' up and going to Penuel's to live. And she and little Rhodory would kind o' want somebody along with 'em this winter, because Penuel thinks of going in."

"In? Where?" I asked her.

"Camp. Lumbering. They wouldn't hear from him, maybe, for six months; and then, there'd be no tellin' what first. It's a precious anxious time in the spring, you may believe, amongst the lumbermen's folks, up and down the Kennebec. When the river comes tearin' and ragin' by their doors and windows, day long and night long, straight from where the boys are, as if it *did* bring news; and they can think of nothing else. When they know the big rafts are making, and the log-drivin' beginnin', and the freshets, and the jams; and them that comes home safe'll be most sure to bring some news of trouble for somebody, out of the six months' winter, and the silence, and the danger. I did think I'd ought to be with her."

It was the same love, motherdie! Yours and mine. What could I say, then?

I feel so tender for everybody's mother now; and for all women who are beginning to grow old.

That is what mother, and daughter, and sisterhood, and all, are given for. Little bits of what holds all together. The heart-work and the heart-life of the world. So that all motherliness is *our* mother's, and all child's love and brother's love, or even what might be, is ours. As it was His who said, "Of these who do the Father's will, each is mine, in every tie; each is my brother, and sister, and mother."

I saw it the other day — I wanted to come home and tell you — in a plain, common man; this beautiful recognition; and it warmed my heart for many days.

I was coming out in the car. The conductor was a young, bluff, fresh-faced fellow; and among the passengers was a tidy, comfortable old Scotchwoman. She "wanted to stop at Mrs. M'Ilvery's; a little, low, brown house with a lattice-work porchway, and steps through it up to the door. Did he know? Just past Grover's Corner."

"All right, mother!" says the young conductor. That touched me to begin with, and made me watch.

By and by, the woman and I, and a little boy who jumped on to the platform, and called the conductor "George," with a great air of pride in the familiarity, were the only people left. And then it came out that she had but ten cents' change to pay her fare, which should be twelve.

"I've got," she said, looking in the young man's honest blue eyes, and putting her hand toward the bosom of her gown, "a bill; it's twenty dollars; but I took ten cents for my fare, for that was all Susannah said it would be."

"Never mind, mother," says George, again. "All right." And took the ten cents.

"I believe," says the Scotchwoman, "you must be from the old country yourself."

"No, I'm a Yankee. We aint all lean kine, mother!"

"What did you call her 'mother' for, George?" whispered the boy, as his friend in authority pulled the strap, and chivalrously helped the old lady down before the latticed porchway, and then sprang on again while the car started. "*She* isn't your mother."

"She's somebody's mother," said George. "And I'm somebody's son. It's all the same. The world's all fathers and mothers and children. Don't you see?"

It was beautiful that *he* saw; and it did me days' good; and in my heart I turned with it to you, as I do with everything.

So I said to Emery Ann, "Why not ask the mother here to spend the winter with you? She and Rhodory can have the little kitchen bedroom, and you can come upstairs."

I felt as if I could do for you, dear, if I only did for "somebody's mother."

And old Mrs. Breckenshaw and the little girl are here; and the house has been pleasant all winter with what ought to be in a home. It has been motherly and daughterly, here, again, for your sake.

Is that taking from the Lord in anything?

When their sakes are his sake, and all the mothers and sisters are his? —

See how I write to you, and tell and ask, as if, somehow, the very words were to go!

My "outings" are all toward you.

Why not? I think that all providings for this life show the providings for the unseen. Did men piece out God's work with their cunning device of letters and messengers, inventing something new under the sun, the pattern of which was not in all the heavens? Or did He put it carefully among the possibilities and intents and the things to be, as He did the oak-seed and the mustard-seed?

I was thinking of it so the other day, when word had just come again from Eliphalet and Gertrude. Of the wonderful thing it is that there should have been a thought and a way put by, against the need of far-separated people to communicate and understand upon the earth; of the strange, possible signs that men were sure to find and put together as they were to speak; and of the great system that grows out of them; of how the whole world is busy sending, carrying, and receiving, and the very air is alive with the rush of its written messages, to and fro.

How it was truly meant and a part of God's plan

and supplement for us; as truly so, as that we should walk about or speak to each other. And everything being but a showing and a parable, it came to me so surely that He will take care of our hearts, and of the spiritual distances; and by his dear providing messages do go to and fro; that the heavenly air is full of loving and helpful and remembering words; and that each soul may get some and may send some every day. "That which is spoken in the ear in closets is heard upon the housetops." Out of God's mails no letter is lost.

That is what I think about what they call "spiritualism" in these days. That it only cumbers itself. That the *thought* is so real and so sure,— that each soul has its own so certain and direct communing,— that this dealing in signs and second-hand is as if, in a land and a time when everybody knows or may know how to write his own letters, the public scriveners should set up their stands, as they did in the old, untaught places and generations. I am afraid men may ask for signs and cling to *them*, and be satisfied; not seeing the *miracle;* not perceiving the inner splendor,

— the real spirit-working; the kingdom of God coming nigh, and already at the doors.

I wish I could put into words some inward perception of this life in which we live. This that we do touch, and breathe, and see; only as with our souls. But they are the "things in heaven above" that we may make no graven image of. They are only spiritually discerned.

I find a word in the New Testament, — a word, indeed, of the New Testament has found me, newly, — a word burning with its own light, and shedding its blaze over all the gospel, from every sentence in which it is put. A word, the letter of which is radiantly one with its spirit; and taken simply in its letter translates to as perfect an image as things can give, the deep, unspeakable truth.

The word is "glory."

A shining Presence.

A lightening forth of that which is always here; the "coming" of which is as the flash "from the one part to the other part under heaven.". The electric fact abides; so does the spiritual. It envelopes us always. When the fine, subtle conditions are met, then, all at once, heaven and earth are full of its brightness. The beginniug of miracles done in Cana of Galilee " manifested it forth ; " and every act and word of the Son of Man reveals it, to that appearing of Him which is and shall be " in the glory of the Father and with his angels."

"Said I not," he asks, " if ye would believe, ye should *see* the glory of God?" Not sign, or wonder, or stroke of power ; but disclosing ; outshining of that which filleth and worketh in all ; the living nearness ; the heaven *in which*, and not up to it from afar, we pray as he has taught us.

That is what " glory " says to me all through the holy pages ; that is the key it is for me to the great invisible ; making it shine out of darkness with every word of truth and every teaching of life ; from the prayer that, holding not a word too much or unavailing, begins with no mere ceremony of address, but with a sentence put into our lips to make us feel all heaven about us, and ourselves face to face with the Father in his holy place, beseeching for his kingdoms of outer and inmost to be both made one, — to the hope of the city that shall have no need of the sun, because the glory of God shall lighten it.

The Easter flowers are in the window; and the Easter joy is in my heart.

I shall not always be blind; I feel what touches me.

Even the Son of Man who came down from heaven and who was in heaven, bore also the conditions of the flesh. Even after his resurrection he had not fully "ascended." He touched that realm as we touch it; it was close and warm about him; he knew that at any moment he might ask of the Father and have twelve legions of angels; yet only now and then they "appeared" out of the glory, strengthening him visibly; or "out of the excellent glory" came the loving, audible voice of God.

Can we not wait as he waited?

Oh, I believe that there is no *away;* that no love, no life, goes ever from us; it goes as He went, that it may come again, deeper and closer and surer; and be with us always, even to the end of the world.

"Out of the body, to God." That shall be the last outgoing; the everlasting entering in.

That is what we wait for,—the adoption; the redemption of our body; the full manifestation of the sons of God.

That is what shall certainly come in my turn, even to me also: the outgoing of the morning; the instant flowering of this life into the larger; the new birthday; and as we found each other here, when this life was to be for us, so surely your face waiting for me there,—

Motherdie.

www.ingramcontent.com/pod-product-compliance
Lightning Source LLC
Chambersburg PA
CBHW021827230426
43669CB00008B/893